M000317928

"There is no greater cause and n
cause than the spreading of the ␣␣␣␣␣␣␣␣␣␣␣␣␣␣␣␣␣␣␣␣␣␣␣␣␣␣␣␣␣
sionary, I know how deeply flawed I am and we are as missionaries and how
much we need prayer. Pastor Eddie is tackling an incredibly important and
strategic task of mobilizing and equipping the saints to pray for missionaries.
Use this book. Share it with others. I highly recommend this important book
for global missions."
Michael Oh, CEO and global executive director of the Lausanne Movement

"Having served in overseas missions for a number of years now, I know how
important it is to have a team of prayer supporters behind you. In this book,
Pastor Eddie gives the reader very practical lessons on how to effectively
support their missionaries in prayer. The personal stories within are illumi-
nating to the real struggles and needs that missionaries face on a daily basis,
and their need for intercessors. *Praying for Your Missionary* is a must have for
churches and missionary supporters. I will be recommending it to all of my
family's supporters in hopes that they will use these guidelines to lift us up
in prayer."
Ryan Klejment-Lavin, director of Footstool Missions Center

"*Praying for Your Missionary* is a great reminder, even for people in full-time
ministry, that we all need to do our part to pray for our field workers. Pastor
Eddie offers insightful, firsthand knowledge of the challenges that many missionaries experience in the field and when they return home. This book should
be required reading for any church that sends and supports missionaries."
Alex Lim, director of Five Two Foundation

"As a crosscultural worker focused on Northeast Asia, I am so grateful that a
pastor has addressed the paramount issue of praying for missionaries. Pastor
Eddie has written a book that is very thorough in addressing so many of the
issues that many workers on the field struggle with. This is a book that I
would want all of my supporting churches and supporters to read. The book
addresses issues for beginning missionaries as well as for those who are ready
to retire. If you know someone on the field and want to understand them, this
is a must read."
Jamie Kim, executive director of Reah International

"Being a missionary in remote places in the world, I greatly appreciate prayer for my family and for our ministry. As Pastor Eddie shares in this book, sometimes our brothers and sisters in Christ forget about us as they do not see us on a day-to-day basis—out of sight, out of mind. People need a reminder to pray for us missionaries as we go out into a dark world to carry the light unto the lost peoples of this world. Pastor Eddie used to be my pastor and our family was greatly blessed by the church and the many ways they supported and encouraged us. He has lived out what is written in this book. As a missionary I would strongly encourage you to read this book and to get it into the hands of everyone in your church to faithfully intercede for all your missionaries."

John Woods, International Mission Board of the Southern Baptist Convention

"This book has the potential to have a powerful and eternal impact in global missions work. If every church lived out what is outlined in this book, then I believe we would see a mighty harvest in missions work among the nations. I have been a missionary overseas for over fifteen years and appreciate the honesty and vulnerability that is shared in *Praying for Your Missionary.* There is a great need among the nations, and there is a great need for more prayer. I hope that churches everywhere will read through this book. Thank you, Pastor Eddie, for writing this. It truly is a gift to us missionaries."

Jim Lyons, missionary in the Middle East

"*Praying for Your Missionary* is a great reminder, even for people in full-time ministry, that we all need to do our part to pray for our field workers. Pastor Eddie offers insightful, firsthand knowledge of the challenges that many missionaries experience in the field and when they return home. This book should be required reading for any church that sends and supports missionaries."

Alex Lim, director of Five Two Foundation

"Comprehensive in scope, Eddie Byun leaves no stone unturned when it comes to fully praying for all aspects of a missionary's life and work. This book is not theory. It is highly practical. As a former long-term missionary myself, as I read chapter to chapter, I could not help but think, 'Right on!'"

Marvin J. Newell, senior vice president, Missio Nexus, author of *Crossing Cultures in Scripture*

"Eddie Byun's new book moves us from casual prayer to engagement in the spiritual battles of missionaries. Each chapter introduces a new dimension of potential personal and ministerial challenges. From the discernment of call to retiring well, Eddie Byun lays the biblical foundation needed to commit to the all-encompassing prayer base our ministry partners need. *Praying for Your Missionary* is a must-read for all pastors, small groups, and individuals who mobilize to pray for their gospel partners. It's a resource to return to over and over again."

Sharon Hoover, director of missions, Centreville Presbyterian Church, Virginia, and author of *Mapping Church Missions*

"When Paul the apostle wrote to the Corinthian church, he reminded them of the hardships he and his team were facing as pioneer missionaries in Asia, and then he voiced confidence that God would deliver him and his team, as the Corinthian believers helped them by their prayers (2 Cor 1:11). Today's missionaries would write the same to us: God will deliver us . . . as you (the church) help us by your prayers. Pastor Eddie writes to show us how to pray—biblically, practically, strategically, and passionately. The servants of Christ around the world need you to read this book so that together we may be part of bringing the good news of Jesus to the nations."

Paul Borthwick, author of *Western Christians in Global Mission*

"This book is a practical guide to intensifying our prayer for people who've left the security, comfort, and familiarity of their old home to journey with others in new places and contexts as we travel together toward our home in the kingdom. Beneath the traditional mission language used in this book is a challenging reframing of our attitude and approach to mission. The author summarizes this through the words of a Ugandan woman: 'I speak as one of many who is no longer prepared to tolerate the narrative of white saviors who are giving it all up to save us.' Mission is no longer (and in truth, never has been) from us to them. Rather it is our privileged participation in the indefatigable love of God as we discover our deep kinship with people whose lives and contexts are radically different than our own—yet share deep dignity and worth as children of God. This book opens myriad specific ways we can pray for all of us to 'watch, stand fast in the faith, be brave, be strong. Let all that you do be done with love' (1 Cor 16:13-14)."

Tim Dearborn, author of *Beyond Duty* and *Short-Term Missions Workbook*

PRAYING

for

YOUR

Missionary

HOW PRAYERS FROM HOME
CAN REACH THE NATIONS

EDDIE BYUN

IVP Books
An imprint of InterVarsity Press
Downers Grove, Illinois

InterVarsity Press
P.O. Box 1400, Downers Grove, IL 60515-1426
ivpress.com
email@ivpress.com

InterVarsity Press® is the book-publishing division of InterVarsity Christian Fellowship/USA®, a movement of students and faculty active on campus at hundreds of universities, colleges, and schools of nursing in the United States of America, and a member movement of the International Fellowship of Evangelical Students. For information about local and regional activities, visit intervarsity.org.

Published in association with the literary agent Don Gates of The Gates Group, the-gates-group.com.

Figure 1, 10/40 Window: Courtesy of June Park.

Cover design: Cindy Kiple
Interior design: Daniel van Loon
Images: blurred abstract background: © surasaki / iStock / Getty Images Plus
    leather armchair: © PaulMaguire / iStock / Getty Images Plus
    watercolor world map: © shoo_arts / iStock / Getty Images Plus

ISBN 978-0-8308-4556-9 (print)
ISBN 978-0-8308-7373-9 (digital)

Printed in the United States of America ∞

InterVarsity Press is committed to ecological stewardship and to the conservation of natural resources in all our operations. This book was printed using sustainably sourced paper.

Library of Congress Cataloging-in-Publication Data
A catalog record for this book is available from the Library of Congress.

P 25 24 23 22 21 20 19 18 17 16 15 14 13 12 11 10 9 8 7 6 5 4 3 2 1

Y 38 37 36 35 34 33 32 31 30 29 28 27 26 25 24 23 22 21 20 19 18

TO MY LORD AND SAVIOR JESUS CHRIST
Thank you for your love for the nations.
Thank you for your love for Korea.
Thank you for saving me.

TO JAMES NOBLE MACKENZIE
One of the first missionaries to Korea who shared the gospel
with my great-great-grandfather and great-grandfather.
Thank you for sharing the gospel with my family many
generations ago. I too am a fruit of your labor. Eternally
thankful for your obedience to the Great Commission.

TO MY SON, ENOCH JUSTUS BYUN
I pray each day that you will grow to be a man of prayer.
May God use your life to be a blessing to the nations.

Contents

Introduction

WHY A BOOK ON PRAYING FOR MISSIONARIES?

I'VE BEEN IN PASTORAL MINISTRY for over twenty-three years now, spanning four countries—America, Canada, Australia, and South Korea. So I know how hard, lonely, and challenging being a pastor can be. I grew up thinking pastors didn't have the same kind of struggles that "regular" people had, but I know now that they bleed, bend, and break just like everyone else. In the early years of my ministry, I never shared the struggles I had with anyone, especially my congregation, because I didn't want them to think I was a weak leader or a spiritually immature pastor. But after I finally got over my ego and reputation, I knew I had to let people in to see the real me—struggles, shortcomings, and all. One way to increase my vulnerability in front of my congregation was to preach a sermon series on the many challenges that pastors face. The angle I took was to teach our church how they could more effectively pray for their pastor.

When I first did that sermon series several years ago, a common response I received from people after the sermons was, "Eddie, you're making me feel so guilty!" (because they weren't praying for me). Far too many congregation members confided in me that they simply forget to pray for me. Some said they thought pastors didn't need prayers because they were so holy and already had a close walk with God. Others said they didn't feel their prayers would make a difference because they felt so spiritually weak. I realized the enemy had done far too good of a job in making the church believe their prayers weren't needed and were powerless. The church believed these lies. There is power in prayer because of the One who hears our prayers. He calls us to pray to him, commune with him, and partner with him in prayer so his kingdom purposes can be realized here on earth, as they are in heaven.

I also felt led to raise prayer support for missionaries. I discovered that we forget to pray for our pastors, who we see each week, how much more do we forget to pray for our missionaries, who we don't see often. In general, it's "out of sight, out of mind." A number of missionaries shared that when they came back to their sending churches they felt discouraged because no one had read their updates, and some congregation members didn't even know who they were. I want this book to be a means of getting our missionaries back on our radar on a daily basis. They need our prayers. They need our support. And this book is a small gift to our missionaries to help increase the prayer coverage from their family, friends, and supporting churches.

We all have a role to play in global missions. We may not all have the *same* role, but we do have *a* role. God calls many to go to the nations as they declare and demonstrate the gospel of Jesus Christ. God also calls others to support those who go by giving financially, praying faithfully, and supporting creatively. I discovered quite early on in my ministry that if I wasn't going to be sent overseas as a missionary, then my role would be to support missionaries and do my best to send out missionaries from the churches I would be pastoring. Through this book I want to raise up more prayer support for missionaries whose lives have been dedicated to bringing the gospel to the world's unreached places.

Another reason for this book is that I want to go home—to heaven. Jesus tells us in Matthew 24:14, "This gospel of the kingdom will be proclaimed throughout the whole world as a testimony to all nations, and then the end will come." The end of this world and the beginning of our glory with Jesus is connected to the completion of Jesus' Great Commission (Matthew 28:18-20). For this to happen, we need more missionaries and more support for our missionaries so they will have the strength, resources, partnerships, and joy to last their whole lives. They will be more effective with more prayer. And I want to do my part in providing that help.

MISSIONS CARE

I use the acronym MISSIONS CARE to outline the chapters of this book. *M* stands for the need to pray for "more workers"; *I* stands for the need to pray for "intimacy with God"; and so forth. Each chapter covers an important area of a missionary's life or ministry that needs our prayers. Some topics will be more obvious than others, but all are crucial. Therefore, it is vital to keep each part in our prayers. I talked to a number of missionaries who read my book *Praying for Your Pastor* and discovered missionaries have a lot of similar prayer requests, but they also have unique needs that require prayer. After discussions with them through Skype, email, and in person, I learned that the church needs to be more effective in interceding for missionaries. These chapters are the result of many conversations with missionaries throughout the world who shared their honest struggles and challenges of doing ministry in their new countries, which we'll refer to as their mission fields.

I've also included discussion questions at the end of each chapter to help facilitate interaction in a small group setting. I encourage you to read this book together in your church small groups. I also provide a few prayer points at the end of each chapter to help guide more specific prayers for that particular topic. Last, there are action points to help us find ways to bring even more concrete forms of encouragement to our missionaries.

As you engage with God's heart in prayer for these missionaries, don't be surprised if you begin seeing changes in your own life as well. Blessings always come into our lives as we pray. The greatest blessing is time spent in the presence of our King. May you gain more of God's heart and delight in it as you pray through this book.

DISCUSSION QUESTIONS

- Do you struggle with thoughts that your prayers are insignificant or powerless? Do you believe that this can be a form of spiritual warfare? How so?

- What ways can we keep our missionaries in our minds and prayers?

- What countries are being supported through the missions efforts in your church? Commit to praying for those nations as well.

PRAYER POINTS

- First, let's repent of any prayerlessness and ask God to increase prayers for your church's missionaries.

- Pray that God would give you his heart for the lost, the nations, and his missionaries during this study.

- Pray for God to transform your church to be a greater praying church throughout these coming weeks as you pray through this book.

ACTION PLAN

- Search for the names of all the missionaries your church supports and commit to praying for them and the nations they serve in.

- With approval from the church leadership, consider adopting a missionary family as a small group and commit to supporting them.

- Find the place in your church facilities where your missionaries are recognized. Go to that place and pray for them as you look at their photos.

1

Pray for More Workers to Finish the Mission

MATTHEW 9:35-38

MY STOMACH WAS HURTING from laughing so much. Amir kept doing his impersonations of famous American actors and presidents with great accuracy. He was a gifted entertainer! I had only known Amir for three days, but he opened up his home and his life to me. Whenever we were waiting for his wife to finish making lunch, he would act out scenes from famous Hollywood movies and leave us in tears with laughter. I couldn't get over how kind he was. Amir fed me like a king and loved me like family. He didn't know the Lord yet, but his heart was so open I sensed it was only a matter of time before he received Jesus as his Lord and Savior.

After leaving Amir's home, my friend Amy, who was a missionary in that city, said to me, "Eddie, I wish you could be here serving with me and our team. You connected with Amir and the other men in ways I never could because I'm a female. Their hearts are so open right now, but there are so few believers here."

Amy and her team had been in this part of the Middle East for the past two years building relationships with the women of the area. She was noticing how the Spirit had been opening many hearts to the gospel in ways that were never seen before. But unfortunately she knew of only ten believers in that city, and four of them were the missionaries on her team—and they were all female. I returned home with a new resolve to not only support Amy's work but to challenge our church to prayerfully consider being a part of Amy's team. The harvest was ready, but the workers were few.

So where do we begin? We begin by making sure we keep the main thing the main thing. The first prayer request in this series is to pray for more workers to finish the mission. Part of every church's purpose is to finish the mission Jesus gave us, and that is to make disciples of all nations.

Why do we need to pray for more workers? One reason is because Jesus commands us to. In Matthew 9:37-38, Jesus tells his disciples how huge the harvest is but also how few the workers are. So he tells them to pray to the Lord of the harvest to send out workers to his fields. We must begin with prayer because he asks us to pray.

There also is a great need in this hour for more laborers to love the nations. According to the Joshua Project, there are still 3.14 billion people out of reach of the gospel, and less than 1 percent of Christian resources are directed at reaching the least reached and unengaged people groups of the world.[1] Another study found that there are 4.19 million full-time Christian workers, but 95 percent of them are working in the Christian or reached world.[2] This great call from Jesus and the great need in this hour confirm the importance of having this prayer request as a high priority in our lives.

So we want to pray for more workers, but what kind of workers should we pray for?

WORKERS WITH A PASSION FOR THE KINGDOM

One thing to pray for is that God would raise up and send out workers in the mission field with a passion for the kingdom of God. Matthew 9:35 says, "Jesus went throughout all the cities and villages, teaching in their synagogues and proclaiming the gospel of the kingdom and healing every disease and every affliction." We must pray that God would raise up, release, and unleash people with a burning passion for his name to be known in all the nations.

We live in challenging days. Christians are dying in many parts of the world. Terrorist attacks are spreading throughout Africa, Europe, and into the West. The moral compass of nations is eroding. It can appear bleak, but as people of faith, we do not worry; instead, we pray and trust in a good and sovereign God. As the days grow darker in a world that does not love God, we must pray for the Light of the world to burn brighter through the church.

As Jesus went through all the cities and villages, he was teaching and preaching the kingdom of God. Pray for men and women who have a passion to do the same. Pray for a people whose love for Christ and passion for the kingdom will also bring them to the cities and villages of the world—teaching the kingdom; preaching the gospel; and bringing hope, healing, and love to a broken world. In other words, pray for a people who will declare and demonstrate the gospel through kingdom living. We want to pray for people who understand that their lives are created to be lived for the kingdom of God and to the glory of his name. Pray that in this generation God will revive a people who take the Great Commission seriously and who, as followers of Jesus, want to make the Great Commission great again.

This means we are interceding for God to stir up a people who know that the Great Commission is not optional. We are living in the last days before Jesus returns! Hear the words of Jesus again:

> Jesus came and said to them, "All authority in heaven and on earth has been given to me. Go therefore and make disciples of all nations, baptizing them in the name of the Father and of the Son and of the Holy Spirit, teaching them to observe all that I have commanded you. And behold, I am with you always, to the end of the age." (Matthew 28:18-20)

Pray for a people who *will obey* this call to go! To go! To make disciples of *all* nations, *all* people groups, *all* tribes, and *all* tongues. Since these are some of the final words of Jesus before he ascended to heaven, these last words hold great meaning. He clearly focuses the mission for his followers: "make disciples of all nations." All the nations matter to God! All nations are called to turn from their sins and find life eternal through trusting in the person and work of Jesus Christ. That is why we must pray for workers who have a passion for his kingdom.

The enemy seeks to diminish our kingdom passion by tempting us to stay in our comfort zones. The temptation to pursue the American dream: pampering, prosperity, and white picket fences. Sometimes I wonder if the American dream is heaven's nightmare, taking away passion, people, and resources from kingdom advancement. Few things have done more to water down passion for God's kingdom than the lure of building our own kingdom where the throne is a La-Z-Boy chair in the living room, and men dream of building a man cave with multiple big screens while souls perish, angels plead, and God weeps over this generation.

> *Sometimes I wonder if the American dream is heaven's nightmare.*

Few things have done more to weaken affection for God than *affluence*. It's so easy to fall into the lure of comfortable, self-centered living. This is why we must spur one another toward love and good deeds until the day of Christ's return (Hebrews 10:24). We can do this by surrounding ourselves with people who can sharpen our love, character, and passion for Christ—as "iron sharpens iron" (Proverbs 27:17). I'm so thankful for people like my good friend Eddie Kim, who I met in seminary. Whenever we met, I left wanting to love Jesus more. He had a deep love for the Word of God and meticulously studied the original languages. His passion was contagious. His unwavering devotion to the kingdom keeps fanning the flame of my own heart to burn when I want to fade away.

Likewise, let's pray for God to raise up workers in this hour who have an unwavering, single-minded focus and passion to see the name of Jesus known and spread throughout the nations.

Spiritual powers will oppose us, which is why Jesus reminds us in his Great Commission that all authority belongs to him. We need to be reminded of that because life is war. Life is a battle that tends to keep us off our mission with God. It is a battle of faith. It is a battle over what our souls will treasure more. It is a battle because the eternal destiny of souls is one of the highest priorities of God's kingdom. And the only way we will finish Jesus' mission is for God to raise up a generation who will love him more than life, more than death, and more than comfort. Pray for it. And pray that we will be that generation.

WORKERS WITH COMPASSION FOR THE LOST

Another thing to pray is to ask God to raise up people who have a deep love and compassion for the lost. Matthew 9:36 says, "When he saw the crowds, he had compassion for them, because they were harassed and helpless, like sheep without a shepherd." Jesus genuinely cared for those who were spiritually lost. Pray that God would send out workers who have his heart of compassion for those who don't know Jesus. Pray that the church would become concerned for the billions who are harassed and helpless because they are sheep without a shepherd. Pray for

God to send out workers who love people, so that they would not view others as a project to be worked on or a problem to be solved, but as a people to be loved.

Pray that Jesus' compassion would lead us to prioritize life and ministry around reaching unreached peoples. In light of this, we need to familiarize ourselves with two sets of numbers: the 10/40 Window and the 4/14 Window.

The 10/40 Window is the region of the world 10 degrees north to 40 degrees north of the Equator, spanning from Africa to Asia (see fig. 1). It is within this window that the least reached people groups of the world live—those who have never heard the life-saving message of Jesus Christ. In fact, 69.1 percent of all unreached people groups are in the 10/40 window.[3] This is where the largest number of the Muslims, Hindus, and Buddhists live.

We must be not only familiar with and prioritize the 10/40 Window, but we also must prioritize the 4/14 Window.

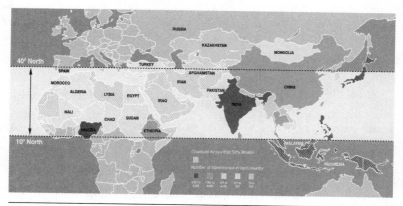

Figure 1. The 10/40 Window

This window represents the ages between four and fourteen, when children are most open to receiving the gospel message. One study found that 85 percent of adult Christians in the United States came to faith in Christ from the ages of four to fourteen.[4] We'd be wise to make these children our priority. When our church was preparing for a church plant in Thailand a few years ago, the 10/40 Window and the 4/14 Window were two key filters determining where we began. We wanted to be in the 10/40 region of the world and knew we placed a high priority on the children in that community.

I also encourage you to become familiar with the Joshua Project (joshuaproject.net), which publishes updates on missions' progress in the least reached parts of the world. Currently there are 6,898 unreached people groups still without a Christian witness. These statistics should affect how we pray, who we pray for, and how we plan and prioritize our missions strategies.

Some of the top unreached people groups right now include

- the Aimaq Taimani of Afghanistan with 0.00% who are evangelical Christians out of a population of 592,000
- the Arab Yemeni in Yemen with more than six million people and no known evangelical Christian population
- the Najdi Bedouin of Iraq: 1.4 million people
- the Tay of Vietnam: 1.7 million people

One of our church members shared with me how her friend from college felt called to go on mission. He looked at the list of least reached people groups from the Joshua Project and simply picked the least reached group on the list. From that point on, he dedicated his life to being a witness to the least reached parts of the world. I was so blessed and challenged by that devotion. Let us pray that God will raise up more people with a passion for his kingdom and compassion for the lost.

Those who love Jesus will do all they can to prepare for his second coming. This means lovers of Jesus need to strategize well to reach this goal. Missions must be put intentionally into his disciples' plans if it's going to be a priority in their lives. Plan to partner in missions through your giving, praying, going, and sending. Plan your vacations around going on mission trips, visiting missionaries, and blessing them. It could be something as simple as babysitting for them so they can have a long-overdue date, or it might be cooking meals for them. Ask how you can help serve them, and commit to being their friend, supporter, and servant for the days that you are there.

A family in our church used their vacation time to visit missionaries our church supported. Though they could have gone to Disneyland or some other vacation destination, they wanted to teach their two young children about the importance of the kingdom of God by serving our missionaries in Thailand. The experience was such a blessing for them that the next year they organized another trip with five other families, and all of them went to serve these missionaries. They were happy to serve, but an added benefit was how the parents and children bonded as they served together for the first time in their lives.

It's also important to plan your giving around missions. Tithe to your local church, but also get in the habit of giving a portion of your income to missions on a regular basis. Some of you might be thinking, *I can't give to missions! I don't have that much money.*

But did you know

- If you make $1,500 in a year, you are part of the richest 20 percent in the world?

- If you make $25,000 a year, you are the richest 10 percent of the world?

- If you make $50,000 a year, you are the richest 1 percent in the world?[5]

We are a wealthy generation. But instead of planning for our giving, we more often dig through our cars and pockets and sofas for loose change and then say, "Here, God! All for you! Use it to the save the world!" But those transformed by grace understand that *all* we have is from God and belongs to God. And all of it is to be used for the glory of God.

We must also learn to plan our future around missions: our next contract, our career, and even our sabbatical. It has been said that missionaries are simply doing what God has called them to do, with the gifts he gave them to use, in a place where there are no Christians. I've been pastoring an expat congregation in South Korea for the past eight years, and I repeatedly give this challenge to our congregation. I tell them, "When your work contracts expire, don't assume that your home country is your default destination. Instead, pray about doing the same job you did before but in a country that needs a Christian witness." I was thrilled to see many people taking this challenge. We had one couple who were English teachers in South Korea. As their two-year contract to teach was coming to an end, they looked for teaching opportunities in other parts of the 10/40 Window and ended up moving to a country in the Middle East to teach *and* to be witnesses. Others responded as well, with several moving to Thailand and Cambodia, and others going to different parts of the Middle East. It was exciting to see them living for the mission of God.

Another thing to consider is tithing not just your money but also your life to the Lord. I've heard many people say, "I'll wait until I retire and then I'll give those years to the Lord." We don't know when God will take us home, so why not prayerfully see how God wants to use your life *now*? How about tithing six, seven, or eight years of your life to God—living, working, and serving in nations where few know Jesus? Several years in Thailand, Cambodia, Vietnam, or Iran. That's not a waste of life; that's an investment of life that honors Jesus as worthy of it all. That may not be a viable option for many, but I know God is calling some to make that kind of sacrifice for Christ and his kingdom.

Just as the breaking of the alabaster jar was wasteful to the world but sweet worship to Jesus (Mark 14:3), so is a life that gladly gives it all for him. Give your life, your degrees, your careers completely as an offering to Jesus. Declare to him, "Here, God, this is yours! Use it all for your glory. It's all for you." Pray for this kind of heart and these kinds of workers to be released into the nations.

Having grown up a lifelong Chicago Cubs fan, the 2016 baseball season was an incredible journey. When it looked like the Cubs were going to make the postseason and possibly win their first World Series championship since 1908, a number of my friends asked me if I would be okay if Jesus came back right before the Cubs won it all. Some friends replied, "Hmm, that's a tough one." Now, I know the question and even the response were just a joke, but sadly for a lot of Christians today, that *would* be a tough decision. It's a difficult decision because our love for sports, games, and personal pursuits are in competition with our love for Jesus.

We need to pray for a people whose love for Jesus and for the lost burns brighter than their love for anything in this world, because those who love Jesus long for his return. And if reaching the nations with the gospel will signal the return of Jesus, then our priority must be to reach the nations with the gospel. Pray that this generation will be the one that completes the Great Commission.

WORKERS WITH INTERCESSION AS A PRIORITY

One more thing to pray for concerning the kind of workers to be sent out is that they would be people who put prayer as a priority in their lives. Matthew 9:37-38 says, "Then he said to his disciples, 'The harvest is plentiful, but the laborers are few; therefore pray earnestly to the Lord of the harvest to send out laborers into his harvest.'" Jesus declares the great need for people to get on mission with God, therefore pray! He doesn't say, the need is huge, so hurry up and get out there! He says pray. Pray and ask the Lord of the harvest to send out laborers into his harvest fields. So before we go to the nations, we are to go before the throne of God and intercede for the nations.

We must pray for missionaries who prioritize prayer in their lives. Why? *Because prayer and missions go hand in hand.* I don't think it's a coincidence that at the peak of the Korean church's influence around the world it was known for its prayer and missions. In a place of prayer and worship Isaiah saw a vision in Isaiah 6, and from that place before God he received his call to go and be the Lord's messenger.

And later on in Isaiah 56:7 the Lord says,

> These I will bring to my holy mountain,
>   and make them joyful in my house of prayer;
> their burnt offerings and their sacrifices
>   will be accepted on my altar;
> for my house shall be called a house of prayer
>   for all peoples.

God's house will be called a house of prayer for all nations. Prayer and mission are connected in the kingdom of God because those who dwell in his presence gain his heart and receive his assignments. His heart cries out for the lost to know saving grace. So pray for people to pray for the nations.

PRAYER IS THE COMMUNICATION
LINE IN THIS BATTLE FOR SOULS

In his book *Desiring God*, John Piper refers to prayer as a wartime walkie-talkie calling in troops and asking for protection. But we don't seem to use it that way anymore.

> Could it be that many of our problems with prayer and much of our weakness in prayer come from the fact that we are not all on active duty, and yet we try and use the transmitter? We have taken a wartime walkie-talkie and tried to turn it into a civilian intercom to call the servants for another cushion in the den.[6]

That is why we must pray for workers who understand that we are not yet home. Instead, may they live in such a way that prayer becomes their home.

The following are a couple of excellent tools that can help increase your prayers for missions:

Operation World.[7] This is a prayer book published by Inter-Varsity Press that guides us through praying for every country in the world. I have used this for many years for my personal prayer times. We have used it in our church too. I make this a required resource to pray through for everyone going on short-term and long-term mission trips for our church. A version is also available online (operationworld.org).

Global Prayer Digest. This daily prayer guide highlights an unreached people group to pray for each day. You can order a physical copy or view it online (globalprayerdigest.org). I learned about this resource through a John Piper sermon. He encouraged families to use this during family devotions. Read through the story of an unreached people group and have your children become involved in interceding for them. It will help them grow in prayer and also grow a heart for missions.

I encourage you to use both of these resources. Your prayers will impact lives for eternity.

DISCUSSION QUESTIONS

- Do you agree with the author's statement that "sometimes the American dream is heaven's nightmare"? What do you think he means by this statement?

- Does sending more workers into the mission field mean simply sending more traditional missionaries? Who else would be considered workers?

- Why are the 10/40 and 4/14 Windows so important for missions work?

PRAYER POINTS

- Ask God to give your missionaries increased passion for the kingdom and the lost.

- Pray that God would send out more workers specifically to the unreached and unengaged parts of the world. Pray for God to send many to the 10/40 and 4/14 Windows of the world.

- Ask God to increase your and your church's financial giving for missions.

ACTION PLAN

- Print a map of the 10/40 Window (or visit eddiebyun.com to download a graphic), put it in your Bible, and begin praying for the nations located on the map.

- If you're not serving in a ministry at church, prayerfully consider serving with children age four to fourteen in order to minister to this important age group.

- Buy a copy of *Operation World* or *Global Prayer Digest* and begin praying through those important resources. Also consider buying a copy for your church library if it doesn't have one.

2

Pray for Intimacy with God

MARK 3:14

WE ARE CREATED FOR INTIMACY. We are created to be deeply known by others and to know others deeply. When that is missing, a longing grows in our hearts. We see it clearly in babies and children. When my son Enoch was a young toddler, whenever he was tired, scared, or not feeling well, he wanted to be in my arms. Even though he's getting bigger and heavier (as I write this he's five and weighs a healthy 20 kilograms [44 pounds]), I love having him in my arms. Each time I pick him up from preschool, I love to hoist him up, spin him around, and give him a kiss. I'm sad the time is coming when he'll be too big for me to hold, but his need to be close to his earthly father and to his heavenly father will always be there. That need continues even when we become adults. It's true for all children of God, and it's true for missionaries as well.

The challenge we face can be understood by something a missionary once said to me: "It's so easy to take our relationship with God for granted because we're doing ministry and we're on the front lines. The irony of it is that I think because I'm doing his work, it's okay to neglect my personal time with him." It's easy for us to take this for granted as well, but we'll look at how we can address it in the place of prayer.

PRAY FOR HEARTS THAT PAUSE
BEFORE THE LORD

We need to pray that missionaries will have hearts that will pause and be still before the Lord every day of their lives. One missionary shared, "Sometimes I wake up and hit the ground running, but what I need to do is hit the floor praying." We must pray that missionaries never forget their primary call. Why did Jesus select his twelve disciples? Mark 3:14 tells us that he appointed the Twelve so "they might *be with him* and he might send them out to preach" (emphasis mine). This is an important reminder for all of us: *being with him* comes before *doing for him.* The first call God has for our lives is to simply come to him. This is for every believer—the missionary, the mom, the mechanic. Jesus invites us all to come to him so he might give us rest (Matthew 11:28).

He tells us to bring our burdens to him so we can carry them together. This is crucial for our spiritual lives because our souls find rest in God alone. Being comes before doing. Otherwise, we'll grow weary. Worship comes before working. Sitting comes before serving. Loving comes before leading. When we give for God more than we receive from God, it means we're running on empty, doing things in the power of the flesh instead of the power of the Spirit. That eventually leads to burnout. So we must pray for hearts that pause before the Lord each day. First Thessalonians 5:9-10 declares, "God has not destined us for wrath, but to obtain salvation through our Lord Jesus Christ, who died for us so that whether we are awake or asleep *we might live with him*" (emphasis mine). Jesus died for us so we might live with him. We need to be reminded of this often, and so do our missionaries. Jesus loves you. He wants to be with you. Today and forever. That's why he died. Deep, daily enjoyment of God is how missionaries are born and sustained.

This is an important prayer request for missionaries because they are so often stressed out. A study was done on the stress levels experienced by missionaries.[1] The test administered is called the Holmes-Rahe Stress Scale, which health professionals use to measure stress in people's lives. According to research, people with a score of 200 will likely have serious long-term health problems within two years. Veteran missionaries maintained levels of more than 600! First-term missionaries were found to have scores peaking at 900. While filling out this stress test, one missionary who scored over 500 didn't include such things as

Deep, daily enjoyment of God is how missionaries are born and sustained.

- almost crashing into someone or something in a truck several times a day on the way to work

- flying small planes onto jungle airstrips, knowing every time he flies, he or a family member might die

- instructing his kids on what to do if a cobra wanders into their yard while they're playing outside

Another missionary from MTW (Mission to the World) shared a glimpse into the many ways that missionaries face stress on a regular basis. She said there were five main categories of stress from crosscultural missions.[2]

Situational factors. Entering a new cultural environment, especially in developing countries, can be very stressful. For some, it can mean stress from something as basic as an increased pollution in the new country. For those who work in places like Japan, frequent earthquakes or typhoons become a challenge. Other issues might include corruption in the new country or the loss of close friendships and feelings of isolation. Some missionaries mentioned things like not having daily access to hot water or even filtered drinking water as sources of daily stress. Another source of stress for some is having things stolen because neighbors think they are rich foreigners.

Daily challenges. Encountering communication difficulties in learning a new language and not understanding things spoken in social settings is stressful. In a group setting when everyone is laughing at a joke except you, it highlights the fact that you're an outsider.

Life events. The cost of being a missionary for some means missing the birth of nieces, nephews, and grandchildren, or the marriages of your best friends. Knowing you can't be there is hard, but then seeing the photos on Facebook additionally pains the heart. Not being there when a loved one is ill or seeing family members grow up and grow old can be a challenge.

Traumatic events. One missionary found the following events traumatic. She had to confront a thief in her home. There were near-fatal accidents almost every day while traveling and taking public transportation and taxis. Seeing poverty surrounding her on a daily basis began to weigh heavily on her heart. And having the government tell her to return home because of the increased threat of terrorism where she served added great amounts of stress.

Personality and gender issues. Female missionaries from the West often find that living in a male-dominated culture overseas can bring a shock to the system. Similarly, being an extroverted woman in a culture where women are expected to be silent is challenging. I was on a mission trip in the Middle East, and during lunch the men and the women were separated—the men ate in the living room and the women stayed in the kitchen. The host brought out a huge dish of chicken with rice and vegetables that could have easily fed twelve people. There were only eight men: five on our team and three nationals. We were stuffed, but our hosts kept insisting we eat more. Unsure of the cultural expectations, we tried to finish all the food so as not to offend our hosts. We almost passed out from eating so much, but we pretty much finished the whole dish.

After lunch we gathered with the women on our team and asked them if they were as stuffed as we were from lunch. We assumed that they were also given the same kind of dish we had. We didn't know that after the guys had finished eating, the leftovers were given to the women! We felt so bad for eating so much of it. Had we known that was going to happen, we would have left more food for them! We learned from that experience and made sure we left a lot more food for them in the meals that followed.

CULTURE STRESS

We should be aware of culture stress.[3] This refers to the regular (and continual) stressors that consciously and unconsciously hit a person who is living in a culture different from what they're accustomed to. We're all familiar with the term *culture shock*. But more subtle things can also have an impact. Culture stress can lead to many different ailments such as anxiety, insecurity, fatigue, lack of joy, illnesses, discouragement, fears, anger, irritability, resentment, and homesickness. And if left alone, these factors can lead to missionary burnout. One survey found that up to 47 percent of missionaries leave the mission field during their first five years.[4] One agency said some of their missionaries left the field because of their inability to handle the stress and shock of the new culture. They believed that more could have been done to prevent the missionaries from leaving the field.[5] This is a key reason why their ability to pause daily before God is so important.

One place I experienced culture stress most vividly was Guinea, Africa, where several of my friends were serving as missionaries. Guinea is one of the poorest countries in the world, and though it was once colonized by France, the country's infrastructure was destroyed before they were given independence.

Before pulling out, the French destroyed plumbing lines, water wells, and all the paved streets, basically crippling the country into poverty and making them start from square one as a developing country.

From the moment I arrived, wave after wave of stressors hit me. People told me to try to locate my luggage quickly because it was common for someone to steal luggage. As we walked out, the intense heat and humidity hit me like a thick cloud. Every part of the city was extremely crowded, and everyone was asking for money since they saw us as "rich foreigners." Guinea is a Muslim nation, and the Muslim prayers spoken throughout the day became "surround sound" wherever I went. Those prayers would also wake me up late at night and early in the morning. The roads were so bad that sometimes a mere two-block drive took over thirty minutes! Our final drive from a rural village back into the city took twenty hours. A friend told me that if the road were paved, that trip would've taken just two hours. On our final day there, my friends took us to a beach. It was a refreshing break from the challenges of the past two weeks, until a gang of forty men surrounded our group and demanded we give them money or else. Our host missionaries were able to talk with them and allow us to leave unharmed, but I think those were the two most stress-filled weeks I have ever had.

After the beach incident, my team and I couldn't wait to get to the airport and head back home. But then it hit me. I could leave, but my missionary friends were living there for the long haul. While I couldn't bear the thought of staying there any longer, I was surprised to see how much these missionaries loved it there. Each missionary displayed great joy the whole time we were together. When I mentioned how challenging it must be to live there, they said yes it is a challenge, but they also said the only way they could survive each day was to pause daily before God. Their only way to handle the stress of each day was to close their eyes to their surroundings and be still and know that the Lord is God.

It's so easy for us to get up and get going with the day-to-day tasks we face. But this story is a crucial reminder for us to pray that missionaries will be able to pause before God often and let his presence in prayer become their home. That kind of praying becomes a great gift to give to missionaries. We must never forget that intimacy with God is what strengthens our weary bodies and souls. "He appointed twelve (whom he also named apostles) so that they might be with him and he might send them out to preach" (Mark 3:14). God called them (and us) first and foremost to be with him.

PRAY FOR HEARTS THAT PURSUE THE LORD

Another thing to pray for to help missionaries' intimacy with God is hearts that pursue the Lord. Psalm 119:9-11 says,

> How can a young person stay on the path of purity?
>> By living according to your word.
> I seek you with all my heart;
>> do not let me stray from your commands.
> I have hidden your word in my heart
>> that I might not sin against you. (NIV)

The first and last lines are the famous parts of these verses, but the middle line reveals the heart behind those verses. The psalmist cries out, "I seek you with all my heart."

A primary way we seek God is through time spent in his Word—reading it, studying it, and storing it in our hearts. So we pray that we and the missionaries in our lives will stay hungry for the Word of God. This is such an important prayer for those whose professions involve the Word of God because knowledge by itself is dangerous. Paul tells us that knowledge puffs up but love builds up (1 Corinthians 8:1).

When teaching at seminary, I tell my students that a common danger of studying in seminary and doing homework from the Bible is that we might view the Bible as a textbook instead of the living Word of God. Another danger for preachers and missionaries especially is approaching the Bible merely to get things ready for sermons or Bible studies instead of letting it speak to us, sharpen us, rebuke us, and refine us. So pray for a hunger that leads hearts to pursue God. Pray that our missionaries will run to God daily and rest before him. It's a daily pursuit.

Having lived in South Korea for the past eight years, I've learned that Korean guys know how to pursue someone. Korean dramas are popular among women around the world because they love to see guys pursue their dream girl. Through their persistence, through their giving of one hundred roses for a hundred days of dating (a hundred roses!), and through their willingness to dress up in matching outfits for the love of their life, guys are well known for their pursuing heart.

Whether it is in the realm of dating or in marriage, we pursue the person we love. We desire our beloved. This holds true for our love relationship with God as well. Psalm 122:1 says, "I was glad when they said to me, / 'Let us go to the house of the LORD!'" Lovers of God pursue God.

Our relationship with God is first and foremost a *relationship*, and like all relationships, we must invest in it or it will weaken. I like to compare the marriage relationship to a garden. When we tend to each other's needs, we are caring for the garden. But when we ignore that garden, it's only a matter of time before weeds and thorns begin to grow. I've counseled some couples who have neglected their garden, and it looks more like a dark forest; each step in it is painful because of the weeds and thorns. And our relationship with God needs some tending. So let us pray for a vital relationship with God to be the mark of our missionaries. May all of us pursue the Lord for all our days.

PRAY FOR HEARTS THAT FIND
PLEASURE IN THE LORD

Regarding missionaries' intimacy with God, let's pray for hearts that find pleasure in the Lord. It's one thing to rest in him and one thing to run to him, but it's another thing to *delight* in him! All Christians need to grow in their friendship with God. In Exodus 33:11, we read that "the Lord used to speak to Moses face to face, *as a man speaks to his friend*" (emphasis mine). And in James 2:23, we read that Abraham was called *a friend of God*. God desires friendship with us. And friends enjoy hanging out with each other. We don't have to force friends to be together. And it's an expression of love and an act of worship to find pleasure in God.

One of my favorite quotes on missions comes from John Piper:

> Missions is not the ultimate goal of the church. Worship is. Missions exists because worship doesn't. Worship is ultimate, not missions, because God is ultimate, not man. When this age is over, and the countless millions of the redeemed fall on their faces before the throne of God, missions will be no more. It is a temporary necessity. But worship abides forever.[6]

The aim of our lives and the aim of missions is worship! The exaltation and enjoyment of God in our lives is our ultimate purpose. So if the ultimate aim for missions is worship, then we need missionaries whose hearts are centered on and grounded in the place of worship.

When asked what the greatest commandment is, Jesus responded,

> You shall love the Lord your God with all your heart and with all your soul and with all your mind. This is the great and first commandment. And a second is like it: You shall love your neighbor as yourself. On these two commandments depend all the Law and the Prophets. (Matthew 22:37-40)

All of Scripture hangs on these two commands because the greatest thing we can do is to love God with everything we have. After that, we must love others. The Great Commandment makes the Great Commission possible. Before we are called to go, we are called to come. "Come to me," Jesus says in Matthew 11:28. That is our everyday calling. We are to come to him, abide in him, rest in him, and enjoy him.

The more time we spend with Jesus, the more we fall in love with him because of how great he is and how wonderful his love is. All throughout the psalms, the writers declare his great love (Psalm 57:10; 86:13; 103:11; 108:4). His love becomes our song. His love becomes our strength. Love must be the highest motive of service, which will last until the end, especially through suffering.

Our ultimate motive in missions is not the great need. Our motive is not our guilt. Our motive is that we love Jesus so much, we want others to know him too. And because Jesus loves the nations so much, our desire is to give him what he desires. These motives alone assure that the mission can be completed. And this is how we pray for our missionaries, because nothing matters without intimacy with God.

David Brainerd was a missionary to the Native Americans in New Jersey in the 1740s. And one of the last things he wrote reveals the deepest motive that drove his missions work:

> Friday, October 2. My soul was this day, at turns, sweetly set on God: I longed to be "with him" that I might "behold his glory." ... Oh, that his kingdom might come in the world; that they might all love and glorify him for what he is in himself; and that the blessed Redeemer might "see of

the travail of his soul, and be satisfied." Oh, "come, Lord
Jesus, come quickly!" Amen.[7]

His missions efforts were driven by a love and longing for Jesus.
He wanted others to know the beauty and the glory of the one
who was worthy of it all. May that always be the central motive
in the heart of all our missionaries.

DISCUSSION QUESTIONS

- What are some stressors you have heard your missionaries go through in their countries?

- Have you experienced culture stress before? Give some examples from your life.

- Share how intimacy with the Lord affects how you handle the challenges of life.

PRAYER POINTS

- Ask God to deepen the intimacy your missionaries have with the Lord. Ask God to increase their desire for more of his presence.

- Ask God to help your missionaries to adjust well to the different cultural stresses they will face.

- Pray that their love for God's Word would increase as they read, study, and teach it.

ACTION PLAN

- Write a letter to your missionaries asking them what has been the most stressful and challenging part of adjusting to their new culture.

- As you send that letter, also consider sending a care package with some spiritual resources for them (e.g., sermons, Christian books, Christian music). *Note*: depending on where your missionaries are located, please be aware that sending Christian resources can be a security risk for them, so make sure ahead of time that it would be safe to send it to them.

- After finding out what aspects have caused stress for your missionaries, write those down in your prayer journal and commit to praying for those areas regularly.

3

Pray for Spiritual Coverage

1 PETER 5:8-11

THE CONCEPT OF SPIRITUAL WARFARE often is strange to new Christians. The language of warfare can sound foreign or even threatening. One time I took a team on a short-term mission trip to Thailand. Each evening, we'd have an extended time of prayer, interceding for the nation and for various needs that came up. At the mission base where we were staying, a group of teenagers were visiting from the United States, and one of the girls on the team was coming under spiritual attack each time her team would do a prayer walk, visit a temple, or do street evangelism. A leader from their team asked if we would pray for her that evening. As we were praying for her, she started to scream; it was obvious she was in a spiritual battle. We prayed for over two hours for her deliverance, freedom, and wholeness.

While we were praying, the parents of one of our team members, Sam, called him to check up on him. Like all parents, they were a little worried because their child was away on his first mission trip. They wanted to hear his voice and to be reassured that everything was all right.

In the middle of this intense prayer meeting, Sam said, "Dad! I can't talk right now. Someone's possessed by Satan, and we have to fight against him right now. I'll talk to you later. Bye!" And he hung up. I found out later that his dad was ready to fly to Thailand and take his son home right then and there! It was a new experience for both Sam and his parents, who were not yet Christians. Later on, I had to explain to them what was going on. In the end, they were just glad that their son made it home safe.

Spiritual warfare can be strange to understand, but it is a reality we must come to grips with in our journey of faith. Scripture makes it clear that we *are* in warfare, there *is* a spiritual realm, and we must be ready to fight in this battle by putting on the full armor of God. So as we pray for our missionaries, one of the most important things to pray for is spiritual protection.

I asked a number of missionaries what their biggest prayer needs were, and by far, the number one was prayer for protection. In fact, some of them gave me only one prayer request, and that was for spiritual protection. One of my friends serving in Indonesia said, "Protection is by far the number one request I have. To give an example, for some reason whenever I travel for ministry or go to a new place to preach the gospel, someone in my family always gets sick." Another mentioned that he developed deep depression on the mission field.

Many missionaries feel forgotten. What's sad about that is they are right. We forget to fight for them in prayer, and as a result, many do not finish the mission they started years ago. But we want to change that. We want to establish a church culture that is faithful in praying for our missionaries. Let's commit to that now.

PRAY FOR PROTECTION

All spiritual leaders and those who seek to advance God's kingdom have an enemy seeking to attack them. We must begin by praying for protection over their lives. First Peter 5:8 tells us, "Be sober-minded; be watchful. Your adversary the devil prowls around like a roaring lion, seeking someone to devour." The enemy seeks to devour, destroy, and kill missions work and missionaries. The evil we hear about ISIS—kidnappings, trafficking, rape, and beheadings—point us to dark shadows of demonic influence. It is one way Satan seeks to destroy the nations.

Then 1 Peter 5:9 instructs, "Resist him, firm in your faith, knowing that the same kinds of suffering are being experienced by your brotherhood throughout the world." This reveals something significant to remember. Right after telling us the devil seeks people to devour (v. 8), Peter tell us *how* the devil tries to destroy us (v. 9). And many times, his attack comes in the form of suffering.

Satan is not creative. His methods haven't changed much since the first sin of Adam and Eve. In Genesis, we see these attacks come in the form of suffering. Let's take a look at Joseph's life. Satan's aim was to destroy Joseph through seasons of suffering at the hands of his brothers, who betrayed him; at the hands of Potiphar's wife, who seduced him; and by leaving him in prison. Satan thought he kept God's servant down. But though others may have done those things for evil, God used those things for Joseph's good and for God's glory (Genesis 50:20).

Satan also tried to use suffering to destroy the faith and life of Job. He took away Job's children, his health, and everything in his life in order to kill Job's love for God. But Job loved God more than anything in his life. This is a picture of pure discipleship.

Satan often uses suffering to try to kill our faith and love for Jesus. So we must pray that even though our missionaries suffer, their faith will remain. We must pray for the protection of their faith so that no matter the heartache, the loss, or the disappointment, their faith will remain. After predicting Peter's betrayal, Jesus says, "I have a prayed for you that your faith may not fail" (Luke 22:32).

Later, Peter writes, "After you have suffered a little while, the God of all grace, who has called you to his eternal glory in Christ, will himself restore, confirm, strengthen, and establish you. To him be the dominion forever and ever. Amen" (1 Peter 5:10-11). He is reminding us that our seasons of suffering are only temporary: in a little while Jesus will return, we will be restored, and we can go home.

For the missionary who lost a child to a disease on the mission field or couldn't be there for the birth of their first grandchild or who feels everyone has forgotten her, we must pray that God will protect their faith, that they will love Jesus more than anything in this world.

But we are to pray for protection for their spiritual and physical safety as well. Second Thessalonians 3:1-2 says, "Finally, brothers, pray for us, that the word of the Lord may speed ahead and be honored, as happened among you, and that we may be delivered from wicked and evil men. For not all have faith." The enemy is Satan, but he will often use people as a means of attack. So we must pray for God to protect them from danger and from attacks.

Billy Graham shares this story in his book *Angels: God's Secret Agents* about missionary John Paton and his wife, Mary, who served as missionaries to the New Hebrides people group.

One night, John and Mary "were surrounded by hostile natives who wanted to kill them. They prayed through the night for protection" as their enemies lurked outside. At daylight, the attackers finally began to leave. A year later, the chief of the tribe of the attackers became a Christian, and Paton asked him about the night of the attack and why nothing had happened. The chief was surprised and said it was because of all the men who were there protecting them, hundreds of them in shining garments and with drawn swords.[1]

Meanwhile, in another turn to this story, the Patons' home church had felt a sudden urge to pray for this missionary couple. Only later did they find out that it was at the exact time God had sent the angels to protect them.

Your prayers play a crucial role in the protection and blessing of missionaries, pastors, and leaders.

Your prayers play a crucial role in the protection and blessing of missionaries, pastors, and leaders. God wants to use your prayers to release blessings of protection.

PRAY FOR COURAGE

Concerning spiritual protection, we should also pray for *courage*. We must pray that our missionaries will be filled with courage *from* the Lord and *for* the Lord. In Joshua 1:9 God says, "Have I not commanded you? Be strong and courageous. Do not be frightened, and do not be dismayed, for the LORD your God is with you wherever you go." We need to hear these words of truth over and over again! When the waves of worries and the storms of fear crash over us, we must declare to our souls again, "Be strong and courageous! Do not be frightened! Because the Lord my God is with me wherever I go!" *God is with me! God is for me!* Because I belong to him!

The mission field can be a fearful place. For many of us, just the thought of sharing the gospel with someone next to us on a plane is frightening. But the enemy will use fear to keep us from taking steps of faith and obedience.

Today there is a new reality. Terrorism is spreading in key areas of missions work where the gospel is desperately needed. Spiritual warfare surrounds us, but in some parts of the world the tactics of the enemy are much more evident than others. Now more than ever we must pray for courage for our brothers and sisters on the mission field. We must pray for courage that we will love Christ more than our own lives. We must pray that the heart of this generation will follow the heart of martyred missionary Jim Elliot, who said, "He is no fool who gives what he cannot keep to gain that which he cannot lose."[2]

The apostle Paul says, "Finally, be strong in the Lord and in the strength of his might. Put on the whole armor of God, that you may be able to stand against the schemes of the devil" (Ephesians 6:10-11). Paul reminds us that our strength and our courage come from and are found in the Lord. And he reminds us that we need this courage and strength for the battle we face.

In 1 Corinthians 16:13, Paul writes, "Be on your guard; stand firm in the faith, be courageous, be strong" (NIV). Be bold! Be strong. He's saying they can no longer approach spiritual warfare as if they were children. It's time to grow up. It's time to be bold, be strong, and do what God has called us to do. It's time to put our childish ways and childish toys behind us. It's time to repent of the delayed adolescence of this generation and enter into the path toward maturity, responsibility, sacrifice, and courage.

The quality of the person one serves with on the mission field is important. I took a team to Thailand, and at the last minute the trustworthy missionary I was going to work with had a family emergency and couldn't host us. So he connected us with another missionary instead.

This new missionary, who I'd never met, wanted our team to do street evangelism and pass out gospel tracts to unreached neighborhoods. That's fine, except the neighborhoods he took us to had about sixty stray dogs roaming in packs. Every time we turned a corner, another pack of dogs was waiting for us, barking, growling, and chasing us! It didn't help that this missionary stayed in his truck, safe and sound, and told us, "I'll meet you on the other side of town!" I was pretty upset that he put our team in that kind of a dangerous position.

We were stuck with tracts in our hands, dogs in front of us, and nowhere to go. So we prayed for protection and courage, and God supplied it. We smashed stones in front of us as we prayed loudly and rebuked the dogs in Jesus' name! I figured if God could shut the mouths of lions for Daniel, God could do the same with these dogs. We prayed, rebuked, threw stones, and shared the gospel. (Not my usual list of events on a mission trip.) Finally, when we reached the other side of the town, we saw the missionary and were able to head back to our base. Needless to say, I never worked with that missionary again.

However, that experience revealed the kind of warfare we are in and the kind of courage we need to pray for concerning our missionaries. They too may have dogs to get through. But more than that, they face demons that will release hounds into their lives. So they need our prayers for courage.

PRAY FOR ARMOR

Concerning spiritual coverage, we must pray for the spiritual armor of God. Paul reminds us, "We do not wrestle against flesh and blood, but against the rulers, against the authorities, against the cosmic powers over this present darkness, against the spiritual forces of evil in the heavenly places" (Ephesians 6:12). We must remember that our true fight is not against humans but against the spiritual forces that oppose our Savior. We are in a cosmic fight in the spiritual realm. It is a fight for the souls of humankind.

But Jesus has already won this battle! Satan has lost, but he will do all he can to drag as many people down with him as possible. He will attack anyone seeking to make the name of Jesus known to people who know him not. That means missionaries are key targets of the enemy. It's no wonder that in some parts of the world three out of four missionaries won't finish their careers as missionaries.[3] That is why Paul admonishes, "Therefore take up the whole armor of God, that you may be able to withstand in the evil day, and having done all, to stand firm" (Ephesians 6:13). Spiritual armor is the only way we will stand against the enemy. So we must pray for the armor of God for our missionaries.

Pray for the belt of truth to be secure around their waist.

Pray for the breastplate of righteousness to guard their hearts.

Pray for their feet to be ready to go and share the gospel wherever God leads.

Pray for the shield of faith to protect them from all the flaming arrows of the enemy.

Pray for the helmet of salvation to be secure in their minds.

> *We are in a cosmic fight in the spiritual realm. It is a fight for the souls of humankind.*

Pray for the sword of the Spirit, which is the Word of God, to be well equipped in their lives, to be a mighty weapon in their arsenal.

Pray that they will be a people of prayer! (see Ephesians 6:14-18).

DISCUSSION QUESTIONS

- What kinds of spiritual warfare do you face in your life? Are there stories of warfare from missionaries you know?

- Is spiritual warfare commonly thought of in your life and discussed in your church? What kind of balance should we strive to have when thinking of life as spiritual warfare?

- Go through each part of the armor of God in Ephesians 6 and discuss why each part of the armor listed is important for the life of a missionary.

PRAYER POINTS

- Ask God to bring strong protection around all of your missionaries.

- Ask God to give them godly courage whenever they face dangers or difficulties.

- Pray through each part of the armor of God found in Ephesians 6 for your missionaries.

ACTION PLAN

- Consider fasting one meal or one day this week, setting aside that time for more intentional prayers of protection for your missionaries.

- Meditate on one part of the armor of God each day this week, and ask God to strengthen that area of your life.

- To practice courage in your own life, prayerfully seek someone to share the gospel with this week.

4

Pray for Strong Singles, Marriages, and Families

1 CORINTHIANS 7:32-35

IT'S BEEN SAID THAT SINGLES spend a lot of their time wishing they were married, and married people spend a lot of time wishing they were single again. I've found this to be true in the mission field as well. A lot of single missionaries I talked to said, "I think if I were married, I could be more effective in ministry." And some married missionaries also confided, "I think if I were single, I'd have time to do more ministry." But both are dangerous mindsets. A common tactic of the enemy is to disrupt every season of our lives, whether we are single or married.

So we want to pray for the relationships of our missionaries and for their seasons of singleness and marriage to be joyful.

PRAY FOR STRENGTH FOR SINGLES

To begin, we want to pray for strength for the single missionaries on the field. Singleness is a gift from God, and marriage is too. But problems arise when we think these gifts are to use as we please, that we are to use these gifts just for ourselves. That's how the world thinks. This is *my* gift, and I can use it for my *own* purposes however I want.

But these gifts are not to be enjoyed only for ourselves. They are given to us so we might serve others. In marriage our spouse is not meant to serve only us, but we are also to serve our spouse. And the couple together are called upon to serve God and others.

And singleness is not a season to do whatever we want, but we are to use our gift of singleness to serve God and his people. This is Paul's advice to singles found in 1 Corinthians 7:32: "I want you to be free from anxieties. The unmarried man is anxious about the things of the Lord, how to please the Lord." Singleness means your whole life can be lived in devotion to the Lord. Whether it's just for a season or for your whole life, that is one of the purposes of singleness. Therefore, God's charge to singles is to live for the Lord! Serve the church! Go into the mission field! Be bold! Be strong! Take risks for the kingdom of God. You have more freedom to do these things than the married do, so use this gift to go all out for God.

Paul says,

The married man is anxious about worldly things, how to please his wife, and his interests are divided. And the unmarried or betrothed woman is anxious about the things of the Lord, how to be holy in body and spirit. But the married

woman is anxious about worldly things, how to please her
husband. I say this for your own benefit, not to lay any re-
straint upon you, but to promote good order and to secure
your undivided devotion to the Lord. (1 Corinthians 7:33-35)

Your season of singleness is an opportunity to give complete,
undivided devotion to the Lord. Use it well! Invest it. Don't
waste it.

We are blessed by the lives of people like Amy Carmichael,
a missionary from Ireland who knew from a young age that
she would not get married or have children. But through
her fifty-five years of bringing the gospel to India, hundreds of
children were rescued from sex trafficking and idol sacrifices.
As these children came to know Jesus as their Savior, they
called Amy *Ammai* or "mother" because of the love and care
she showed them.[1]

> *Your season of singleness is an*
> *opportunity to give complete,*
> *undivided devotion to the Lord.*

The single missionary
is blessed to have time
and be available in the
mission field, but it's
not without its share of challenges. A number of single missionaries I talked with shared how life in the mission field is glamorous
at first. The thought of wholehearted devotion to God's work is
what drew them. But when the loneliness kicks in, it gets hard,
very hard. When society pressures them to get married and questions why they aren't yet married or when they will start dating, it
takes its toll.

Many begin thinking, *Maybe I'd be more effective in ministry if I were married.* These struggles get so difficult that I know of a few single missionary women who married Muslim men because of their loneliness and struggles. So it is very important to pray for strength for the single missionaries.

Let me give you three specific ways to pray for strength for singles:

Pray for a strong calling. The glamorous image of mission work will only take a person so far. When things get hard, only God's call will keep a missionary on the mission field. There must be a clear call to missions, and for some it will also involve a call to a season of singleness.

Pray for strong contentment (for the single). The enemy will use discontentment to cause singles to waste the season they are in. That mindset will make singles miss what God wants to do with them in this season. So pray that singles would be content for the season they are in and run after the Lord with all their might.

Pray for strong community. Pray that God would provide a good community of believers to surround singles. Lonely times can be most difficult for a single missionary. One female missionary in Thailand shared how she loved the work she did throughout the day, but things were hard at dinner. When all the families would go home to eat together, she'd go home to eat alone. It took a toll on her emotionally. The locals often asked her why she wasn't married. This made her feel like something was wrong with her. So she had to remind herself that being single did not mean she was less of a person. Jesus was single, and he was the only perfect person to walk the earth.

So pray for good friendships between men and women, elderly and youth, couples and singles.

When I was in Kenya for my first mission trip during my freshman year in college, I met Isabel, a missionary from the Philippines. She said she struggled with cultural expectations for women to be married by a certain age (she was fifty at the time). It was hard because of the verbal and physical inappropriateness she faced as a woman walking the streets of the city. But the Korean team she worked with in Kenya helped. One guy in particular became closer to her than her own brother. His name was Tae, and he brought much strength and humor to the team.

An older couple on the team, Sung and Min, became like parents to Isabel. With their wisdom and grace, she could go to them for advice or just to vent her frustrations and struggles. One time she was crying in her room because she missed her mother so much, and suddenly she felt the arms of Min surrounding her just as her own mom used to do. This team became her family.

Though Isabel knew she was called to be single, she also knew she was created for community. And God provided it through her team and the local church.

So pray for strength for singles, for they too need our prayers.

PRAY FOR STRENGTH FOR MARRIAGES

We need to pray for specific needs that single missionaries have, and we need to pray for the needs of married couples too. Marriages face many challenges because of ministry pressures. On the mission field marriages experience additional stress in a new culture. As in pastoral ministry, the missionary's marriage must be a priority. So pray that the husband and the wife would learn to deeply love and serve one another. Ephesians 5:25-27 states,

> Husbands, love your wives, as Christ loved the church and gave himself up for her, that he might sanctify her, having cleansed her by the washing of water with the word, so that he might present the church to himself in splendor, without spot or wrinkle or any such thing, that she might be holy and without blemish.

One of the most important roles of a marriage in the mission field is to show others what the love of Jesus looks like by the way the missionaries love each other. How a husband loves his wife shows the watching world how Jesus loves the church. It's been said that if you want to know what kind of husband a man is, look at his wife. What does her face express? What does her heart express? And likewise, how the wife loves the husband will serve as a beautiful testimony to others as to what marriage was supposed to look like.

There is great warfare against marriages in the mission field. A missionary I met in China who I'll call Jim was a key leader of a church-planting group that was extremely successful. The team was growing so much that he had to double his staff almost every year for five years. One staff member, Tracy, was a huge blessing to his marriage and family. Tracy babysat four or five times a week so Jim and his wife, Nancy, could do more mission work. Tracy became part of the family. But the enemy was working behind the scenes in this situation. One day Jim unexpectedly told the group he would be leaving the country. Not only that, he would also be leaving his wife and six children. Jim moved to Canada with Tracy, leaving Nancy and the kids behind to fend for themselves.

What started out as an innocent desire to help each other in ministry turned into an affair that they were able to keep hidden for four years. The enemy used it to bring an end to a marriage and great heartache to the six children. My heart breaks for the wife and for the kids that she is now raising on her own.

I talked with Jim about a year ago, and it was clear his heart and passion have dwindled since the first time we met. He used to be one of the most passionate people I had ever talked to about evangelism, missions, and the kingdom of God. But now his heart has grown cold to God, the gospel, and even to the church. When a younger pastor I was with asked him about missions and seminary, he said, "Seminary and ministry were the biggest waste of time and money in my life." Both the young pastor and I were shocked and saddened to hear his response, and to see the difference in life.

Sadly, I know of six other missionary families who went through almost the same thing. An affair. A divorce. A broken home. Children hurting. All on the mission field. We need to pray for these marriages. May the love between husband and wife on the mission field be protected by our faithful intercession.

Pray that the first priority of ministry for married missionaries would be to love their spouses faithfully. Remember, "Christ loved the church and gave himself up for her . . . that he might present the church to himself in splendor, without spot or wrinkle or any such thing, that she might be holy and without blemish." Husbands, this is how we are to love our brides, wash them with the Word, and prepare them to meet Jesus! This is a high calling. We are to be Jesus to her. And, wives, let the partnership you share with your husbands be a source of strength for them. Give encouragement and provide support for areas of his weakness.

Our first ministry is to Jesus. Our next ministry is to our spouse and family. Then we are called to the church and the mission. I mentioned earlier how relationships must be cultivated and attended to. And just like with church ministry, mission work can easily dominate a marriage. When that happens, a marriage starts to grow weeds. So pray for missionaries to have marriages growing in love and having fun together.

PRAY FOR STRENGTH FOR FAMILIES

We are to pray for singles, we are to pray for marriages, and we are to pray for the families in the mission field. Pray that the parents will not forget that the first place of making disciples for them is not in the nations but in their homes. Proverbs 22:6 says,

"Train up a child in the way he should go; / even when he is old he will not depart from it." Parents are called to train their children first to know Jesus and to walk in his ways. The seeds we plant in our children at a young age will one day reap a harvest when they grow older.

In Ephesians 6:4, Paul tells us, "Fathers, do not provoke your children to anger, but bring them up in the discipline and instruction of the Lord." But missionary families and kids face many challenges that others may not face as they raise their children.

Growing up as a third-culture kid (TCK) isn't easy.[2] David Pollock explains,

> A Third Culture Kid (TCK) is a person who has spent a significant part of his or her developmental years outside the parents' culture. The TCK frequently builds relationships to all of the cultures, while not having full ownership in any. Although elements from each culture may be assimilated into the TCK's life experience, the sense of belonging is in relationship to others of similar background.[3]

Many TCKs don't have stable friendships because they move around so often. Military kids feel it, and many missionary kids (MKs) feel it too. Not really having a home base is another challenge. One MK said, "I can't go back home because I never really had a home. I don't know what country is my home country anymore. I don't feel at home anywhere." Some of you may feel this struggle as well. But when redeemed, this struggle can be a great source of strength, reminding us that our true home is in heaven.

The lure of workaholism is strong for missionaries too. One missionary pastor in China had to go to different Chinese cities for mission work. One of the cities was a twenty-hour train ride from his home. He eventually got so busy that he was home only on the Chinese New Year to sleep one night, and then headed back to the different cities. He had so much to do, he felt guilty even coming home! Last year, as he was about to board the train to leave his family, his youngest son ran after him, crying and begging him, "Please stay here, Daddy!"

This father kicked his son and said to him, "Get behind me, Devil!" He then pushed his son away and boarded the train.[4]

That may sound extreme, but unfortunately that attitude is far too common. I've talked to far too many ministers who think that it's okay to sacrifice marriages and children "for the sake of the ministry." But when we do this, we are not sacrificing them to God but to the idols of ministry, for our egos and not for the glory of God.

Like all parents, parents on the mission field also struggle with important concerns. They worry about the health, education, friendships, and futures of their children. So we should cover these areas of their lives as we pray. We need the church to be faithful in prayer for missionaries and their families.

Joshua was a missionary in Vietnam for almost twenty years. He married his high school sweetheart, and they had three daughters. But about ten years ago, Joshua started struggling with depression. It got so bad that he had to be hospitalized for months at a time. His wife, Nicole, led most of the ministries while he was away. But the depression worsened, and his stays in the hospital increased. After Joshua's most recent release from the hospital, he did fine for almost three months. He thought things were finally back on track until one day Nicole told him she couldn't handle it anymore and wanted a divorce. This new tragedy only made things worse for Joshua. Months later he discovered Nicole and another missionary from their own team had started a relationship. His world had crumbled. As news of the situation broke out, their mission agency removed them from the field. He was now without his missions work, his daughters, and his marriage. This led to deeper depression for another two years.

Joshua told me that when he first went on mission, he did not realize so many relationships in his life would come under attack. But the attacks came often and in many directions. Even his relationship with his parents took a hit when he told them he was going to Vietnam. They dreamed he would be a wealthy doctor, living a comfortable life. Leaving the United States without their blessing ended their relationship. It took years before Joshua's parents began communicating with him again.

As Joshua started recovering, he met another woman, Beth, who also was recovering from depression at the same hospital. They started to date, and God rekindled their hearts for mission. They married and today are serving in Europe as missionaries. God has blessed them with new children as well.

Joshua knew I was writing this book and said, "Tell the churches to pray for us, Eddie. We want so much to expand

God's kingdom, but we need the prayers of the churches to survive these battles." I said I would tell the churches and that we would pray.

And we will, right?

DISCUSSION QUESTIONS

- Describe what you think the unique opportunities are for singles on the mission field. What unique opportunities do married couples have?

- What would be some unique challenges single people have on the mission field? What about the challenges for married couples?

- Why do you think it's so difficult for us to be content with our present season of life? What do you think we can do to help us be content during those seasons?

PRAYER POINTS

- Pray for God to grant contentment to your missionaries.

- Ask God to deepen the love relationship between all the married missionaries.

- Ask for special protection over the lives of the children of the missionaries. Pray they would know the Lord from a young age and walk with him faithfully for all their days. Pray against any seasons of rebellion and for the deep love of Jesus to mark their lives.

ACTION PLAN

- Write a prayer for the single missionaries in your life. In that prayer, speak blessings and encouragement to them, letting them know how much they mean to you. Then send the letter to them.

- Record in your calendar the anniversaries of the married missionaries you support. Remember to honor those marriages each year. The next time they're in town, give them a date night for them to celebrate.

- Find the birthdays of the missionary children you support and send birthday cards and gifts for them.

5

Pray for Incarnational Love for the Nations

PHILIPPIANS 2:5-11

JACK WAS ABOUT to be a new missionary in Egypt. Having been trained for years, he was finally ready to leave the United States for the Middle East. He was so excited. Since he heard that they had limited seminary training, he couldn't wait to train the Christians and church leaders there. He wanted to bring the gospel and see change in that region. And out of excitement for his new mission field, he asked an elderly Christian from the Middle East for one piece of advice. The elderly man said, "If you want to be effective, go to Egypt and find an Egyptian pastor, and be discipled by him for five years. Then you can begin your missions work."

Jack was offended by that advice. He thought, *What? Are you kidding me? Me, be discipled by them? I'm the one who went to seminary to be trained and then trained again with my missions agency. I'm ready to disciple them!* But he told me after ten years in the Middle East that he should've started with the elderly man's advice. He said, "I saw myself as their savior instead of their servant to point them to the Savior. And the best way I could've been that is to do what I was first told to do—and that was to become a servant and leave the saving to Jesus."

How do we avoid this blind spot in missions? How can we guard our hearts from seeing ourselves as the savior instead of Jesus Christ? A key factor is to pray for incarnational love. This is a great challenge for us who grew up in the West, especially the United States. Our need to pray for incarnational love is often overlooked, so we want to cover ourselves and our missionaries with this important prayer topic.

PRAY THEY WOULD LEAVE THEIR
HOME BECAUSE OF LOVE

The greatest motive that will sustain the missionary is love. As Jesus says, "You shall love the Lord your God with all your heart and with all your soul and with all your mind" (Matthew 22:37). Our motive for missions must come from a love for God. Because we love Jesus, we desire to make him known. Because we love Jesus, we desire others to love him. And we desire to obey his Great Commission: "Go therefore and make disciples of all nations, baptizing them in the name of the Father and of the Son and of the Holy Spirit, teaching them to observe all that I have commanded you. And behold, I am with you always, to the end of the age" (Matthew 28:19-20). What is the connection between our love for Jesus and obeying his commission? Jesus says, "If you love me, you will keep my commandments"

(John 14:15). We keep his commandments to love God and others and to fulfill his Great Commission. When we love someone, we want to honor them, please them, and stay in peace with them. The natural overflow of love is a desire to make the beloved happy.

When God called Abraham to leave his country, his family, and his people, Abraham did not know where he was headed. God just said go, leave your comfort zone. Abraham obeyed. And this same love for his Father led Jesus to leave heaven. Paul tells us in Philippians 2:5-7 that we are to have this same attitude:

> Have this mind among yourselves, which is yours in Christ Jesus, who, though he was in the form of God, did not count equality with God a thing to be grasped, but emptied himself, by taking the form of a servant, being born in the likeness of men.

Out of love, Jesus left the glory of heaven. And in his incarnational love he became fully human, dwelled with us, lived with us, loved us, and ultimately died for us. This is humility. This is love.

God may have called some of you to the city or country that you are in today for that same reason. God may be asking you to empty yourself of your own dreams and to embrace what Jesus loves in that city. There's a comfort in your hometown that you may not have where you are today. There are foods you like better there than where you are now. But you also know that God has called you there for a season and a reason. But the ultimate reason is grounded in love for God.

One missionary friend I talked to said that when he first went to the mission field he was all wide-eyed and filled with excitement. But on his arrival to this new city an older missionary warned him, "You're going to meet a lot of unhappy missionaries here. Just warning you ahead of time."

He met many of the missionaries from the team that afternoon over lunch, then for fellowship, and later for dinner. Sadly, he discovered that the man who warned him was right. Most of the missionaries he interacted with that day were bitter and angry. They were there now because they *had* to be there. They were too old for a career change, so they felt stuck in this career path. Many felt like they had missed out on what their lives could have been. People back home no longer looked up to them as spiritual heroes, if they remembered them at all.

Only a foundation based on a love for Jesus will have the strength to keep a missionary on the mission field with joy. Moving to a new culture to be a missionary for any other reason will end in failure. Because it will require a lot of sacrifice, love for Christ must be the motive.

Pray people will leave their homes, friends, families, and comfort zones because they love Jesus.

PRAY FOR CULTURAL SENSITIVITY

Cultural sensitivity is another prayer item related to incarnational love. Revelation 5:9 says:

> They sang a new song, saying,
> "Worthy are you to take the scroll

and to open its seals,

for you were slain, and by your blood you

ransomed people for God

from every tribe and language and people and

nation."

This amazing verse tells us God will preserve every culture, language, and people group for all of eternity. Heaven will not be just one people or one language or one culture. English will not be the main language of heaven. (I know this might be a surprise to some people.) God will redeem, restore, and celebrate the many different nations that he created.

So this biblical understanding must be the filter through which we do crosscultural missions. We are by nature ethnocentric in how we interact with other cultures. We naturally assume our way is the right way (or the better way). For example, when we look at what annoys us about a new country, we always compare it with our home culture. When we wait in a long line and suddenly see an elderly lady cut to the front, we get mad! How rude!

When an older man knocks someone over to get that seat on the subway, we think, *What a jerk!* But we are evaluating it on the basis of our standards, rarely considering cultural differences. South Korea is a culture in which the older generation lived through war and famine and needed to be in survival mode all the time.

As an American I had to repent of my attitude when I first came to South Korea, thinking that the United States was the best country in the world or that the world revolved around it.

A real eye-opener for me was experiencing 9/11 outside of the United States. Like all others who lived through that horrific day, I remember exactly where I was and what I was doing. It was evening in South Korea when I got a phone call from one of my students. She was hysterical and asked me if the world was coming to an end. I was confused by her question, and then she asked if I'd seen the news and told me to turn the TV on. I did at once, and like millions of others that day, I was glued to the TV, watching the images of the towers burning and eventually falling.

I was stunned and saddened. But in the days to come, I began hearing conversations of people from many different countries who had a surprising response to the events of 9/11. Some said, "The United States had it coming." Or "They deserved it." These comments left me speechless. But as I pressed further, I discovered that many countries do not hold a positive view of the United States. In my ignorance and arrogance, I had assumed every country in the world loved the United States, envied it, and even wished they could live there. I was wrong. Very wrong. I learned that many other countries saw Americans as arrogant and extremely self-absorbed. One person I talked to said, "Americans don't care about any other country. That's why you see these attacks happening." It was a sobering week for me on many levels.

God was teaching me that I had to repent of my self-centered, ethnocentric ways if I was to truly minister to the nations. I continue to apply this lesson as an expat and as a minster serving crossculturally. All missionaries and ministers living and working crossculturally need to be extra careful to honor the culture we are serving. Importing the gospel is too often equated with importing the culture of the missionary.

I've been living and ministering in South Korea for the past nine years. South Korea is considered the greatest missionary success story for the Presbyterian Church. So much of the gospel fruit we see across this land is thanks to the Presbyterian missionaries who over a century ago gave their lives for this country. But as they brought the gospel, they also brought their culture. The Korean people started to dress like Americans (for example, Korean men began wearing Western-style suits instead of traditional Korean clothes). Korean Christians started to use hymnals in worship services. And looking at Korean churches today, regardless of the denomination, you will see the US Presbyterian influence in how they partake in Communion (from the trays used to the robes worn to the gloves they wear to serve). Much of the culture of the West was incorporated into the discipleship of this nation. Not all of it is necessarily bad or wrong, but it shows we need to be careful to honor the culture we are entering and neither dismiss nor discard it.

About a year ago a video of a short-term mission team in Uganda went viral on the internet. It was a mission team from the United States, and it appeared the video wasn't received well by the host country. In response to the video, a Ugandan woman sent the team the following letter:

Dear Dancing Missionaries,

I hope you are OK with that description—it is, after all, how you described yourself on your Facebook page. This week you published a video of your time volunteering with Luket Ministries in Jinja, eastern Uganda. Seven white girls dressed in the Gomesi, the traditional dress of the Baganda tribe, dancing around to "share the joy" you experience "serving overseas on the mission field."

The video came with a disclaimer that it was meant to "make people laugh, not to offend" but maybe that's because deep down you knew it would?

Leaving aside the fact that you joked that "no mosquitos were harmed during the making of this video"—an insect that kills 100,000 Ugandans every year—your fun video openly mocked the day-to-day hardships African women face: traveling long distances to find clean water and carrying their children on their backs while doing hard manual labour.

As a Ugandan woman from the Baganda tribe, the Gomesi is part of my identity and ethnicity. It is part of our rituals during birth, marriage, funerals. It's the nearest an item of clothing can get to being described as sacred.

If you had done any research into the people who welcomed you into their community you would know that a woman dressed in a Gomesi would never display the behaviour you depict in your video: shimmying around to Justin Timberlake's [song] "SexyBack," only with a slight tweak to the lyrics announcing to the world that you are "bringing missions back."

She ended the letter with these sobering words, "Ugandans, and indeed other Africans, have access to the internet and I speak as one of many who is no longer prepared to tolerate the narrative of white saviors who are giving it all up to save us."[1]

Sadly, this is not an isolated event. It is a blind spot that we fall into easily if we do not see nations through a biblical lens. It's not just an issue of maturity that would lead someone to treat a new country in this manner; rather, it is an issue of theology. God created these nations. God loves all nations, all peoples, and all languages.

What do we see in the heart of Jesus? The apostle Paul tells us that Jesus "emptied himself, by taking the form of a servant, being born in the likeness of men. And being found in human form, he humbled himself by becoming obedient to the point of death, even death on a cross" (Philippians 2:7-8). This emptying of ourselves requires humility and obedience to die to ourselves, our rights, and our ideas of what is a "better" culture in order to honor and love the culture we are in.

PRAY FOR DEEP LOVE FOR THE NATIONALS

One more important thing to pray for is a deep love for the peoples of the nation the missionaries are called to serve in. We began this chapter by looking at the Great Commandment as the foundation for missions (to love God). And our love for God overflows into our love for one another (Matthew 22:39).

All of Scripture hangs on these two commandments: love God and love others.

This seems pretty basic, but it's not always our motive. One of my friends shared the story of a missionary in India who said, "I just love my furloughs and sabbaticals! Because those are the times I get to 'wash India off of me.'" When he heard this, he was speechless. Though this missionary spent more than thirty years in India, she never grew to love the people. We need to pray for divine love to be strong in the hearts of our missionaries because their life of service to God is meaningless without love. Paul reminds us of this 1 Corinthians 13:3: "If I give away all I have, and if I deliver up my body to be burned, but have not love, I gain nothing."

If love is not flowing through our veins, our labor is futile. Pray that God would give our missionaries a deep love for the nations and the nationals they serve. Pray for a renewed passion for the souls of the nations. Love for Jesus and love for people must be at the center of their calling.

The biggest change in my life regarding South Korea happened when, out of my love relationship with Jesus, he gave me his heart for that country. I grew up in the suburbs of Chicago as a Korean American, but I fully embraced the American side of my heritage. My friends called me a Twinkie or a banana, yellow on the outside but white on the inside. There was no trace of Korean culture in my veins growing up. So in God's sovereign sense of humor, he sent me to be a pastor in Korea. When I first came to Korea, I must admit that I didn't care anything about Koreans. I figured I was here to reach the expat, English-speaking community, not the Koreans. There were plenty of South Korean churches that could reach the Korean speakers. The largest churches in the world were Korean, so I didn't feel any need to reach out to my Korean neighbors.

But a few years into my time in Korea, God opened my eyes to see the vulnerable who were hurting, abused, and neglected in South Korea, and my love for the country started to grow. Our church began ministries seeking to help trafficking victims; we were active in caring for orphans, widows, single moms, and stateless children.[2] But as I started to preach on these issues and asked South Korean churches to also get involved in caring for them, I met some unexpected responses.

Because the stories of orphans, single moms, and trafficked persons don't give the best impression of a country, some Koreans were offended that I was bringing up these issues in public, and especially on an international stage. A number of times I was even asked by South Korean pastors, "Why do you hate our country so much? If you're going to shame us like that, just leave! Go back to your own country!" (Ironically, as a Korean American, I've been told "Go back to your home country" in both countries.) There were many new cultural lessons I had to learn about why direct speech against some injustices in that nation was culturally taboo. I always tell the Koreans that I speak out against the injustices because I love their nation. But more than that, God loves their nation.

We cannot be silent about the orphan, the trafficked child, or the single mom. We cannot be silent when their hearts cry out for justice day and night. We must join them in their cry, and we must fight for them with the strength, freedom, and resources God has given to us. We are to use all we have for the good of our neighbor and for the glory of God.

We are so selfish on our own. But by God's grace, our hearts are changed to love others. And when that changing work of God's Spirit touches our hearts, we begin to care for the people that Jesus cares for. That's a work of God in our lives. Let's pray for that kind of good work to be done in the hearts of all our missionaries. They need God's grace. And they need our prayers. Let's pray.

DISCUSSION QUESTIONS

- Other than love for the nations, what are some other reasons people might want to become missionaries? List three or four.

- What are some challenges people face when they move to a new country and new culture? How can you help those in your church who have moved from other countries feel more at home and adjust well?

- What are some of the biggest needs in your local community that you as a church can be engaged with?

PRAYER POINTS

- Ask God to send missionaries who are motivated first and foremost out of love for Jesus.

- Ask God to give your missionaries wisdom and cultural sensitivity for the new cultures they have entered. Pray they will be able to build bridges instead of offending locals as they adjust to the new country.

- Pray that God would deepen their love for the nationals they serve, and that God would increase their love for the country and cultures of the people.

ACTION PLAN

- Consider talking with your church's leadership about having a mission festival once a year in which you celebrate the different nations represented in your church. Along with that, consider having different languages being sung during a worship service.

- After one of those special missions services, consider having ethnic foods available for people to try.
- Commit to learning a new culture or studying another country to develop your crosscultural understanding.

6

Pray for Oneness in the Teams

PHILIPPIANS 2:1-4

I USED TO ASSIGN a lot of group projects at the seminary, but the feedback I received from the students made me move away from them. Almost every team would tell me they hated group projects because there always was that one person who didn't do their part and yet got the grade. That's the hard part of not being able to choose your own team. But even if you could pick your team, the sinfulness of the human heart will eventually lead to broken relationships and conflict of one form or another.

In light of that, I always remember the advice of one of my mentors: when you can choose your own team members, there are a few important factors to keep in mind:

- Look at character (does the person have good character and can he or she be trusted?)

- Look for competence (does the person have the ability and skills needed?)

- Look at chemistry (does the person fit the culture of the team? Is there good chemistry with the other team members?)

The biggest challenges to teamwork arise when one of these three elements is missing. But what happens when we don't get to choose who's on our team? How do we maintain unity and oneness? And how do we pray for this concerning our missionaries in team settings?

A missionary named Elizabeth identified four big Ds that are factors in missionaries leaving the field. They are disease, divorce, division, and depression. But from most of the missionaries I spoke with, *division* (or lack of team unity) was the most common challenge. This is crucial.

Let's examine the key things to pray for concerning oneness for missionary teams.

PRAY FOR CLOSE PROXIMITY TO JESUS

Satan attacks in a variety of ways, but one of his favorites is by attacking relationships. When relationships are bad, everything is bad. If there's a strain with someone at work, it's hard being in the same room with that person. When a marriage is going through a difficult season, everything is harder. So in light of this, more than anything else we need a close relationship with Jesus. Sometimes only Jesus can give us the strength to show up to the office. Only Jesus can give us the courage and humility to seek forgiveness in a marriage. And this is true on the mission field. Therefore, it's important to ask God to keep the missionaries in close proximity to Jesus. Pray that each missionary will have a close and intimate walk with the Lord. Relationships are hard. And relationships on the mission field can be even harder. To gain strength and joy to love those around us, we need Jesus.

Paul says in Philippians 2:1, "If there is any encouragement in Christ, any comfort from love, any participation in the Spirit, any affection and sympathy . . ." He's revealing what flows out of a close walk with Christ. He knows that when you spend time with Jesus in his Word, Jesus *will* encourage you! You will be comforted by his love. The fruit of the Spirit will grow in you, and so will affection and sympathy. These are the natural byproducts of a life connected to Christ. These fruits that come from close fellowship with the Lord are the key to protecting the unity of your relationships.

Growing up, one of the few video games I played was *Super Mario Bros.* by Nintendo. It was a simple game guiding a small Italian man through mazes and dodging dangerous obstacles in order to rescue a princess. Though I was never good at that game, I realize there was a lesson we could learn for our spiritual lives. The important lesson is seen in the power supply each life is given. In the game, when I was hurt or shot at or fell, I lost strength. And it was only a matter of time before the game was over and my game lives were gone.

That's a picture of trying to love others in our own power and strength, which is very limited. Think of it as everyone of us having a small Mario man inside of us. As we bump into people and get difficult emails from others, our love capacity depletes quickly! We get that phone call, have that business meeting, or are assigned to a group project with someone who doesn't do their part. Each time, our patience is tested, our hearts are broken, and our love tanks are depleted.

On the mission field the problems are even more intense. And in their situation, an individual's own strength is not enough to love others. The only way we can love other sinners is to be connected to the one who died for sinners. The only way we can handle difficulties in relationships is through a relationship of trust and dependence on Jesus.

Paul informs us, "The fruit of the Spirit is love, joy, peace, patience, kindness, goodness, faithfulness, gentleness, self-control; against such things there is no law" (Galatians 5:22-23). This is the fruit or byproduct of a life that is connected to and ever in need of Christ. How connected are you? Ask yourself, *Do I have love, joy, peace, patience, kindness . . . ?* I can't in good conscience go through this list without getting on my knees and pleading for Christ's mercy and grace and love to fill me again. I need his mercy every day because every day the Mario man inside of me gets quickly depleted of his power to love. This is why we need Jesus. We need close proximity to Jesus every day. So pray for this for you, for me, and for the missionaries.

PRAY FOR UNITY WITH OTHERS

To strengthen missionary teams, it's crucial that we pray for unity with each member on the team. Philippians 2:2 says, "Complete my joy by being of the same mind, having the same love, being in full accord and of one mind." Paul is pleading for unity within the body of Christ. He is telling the church

in Philippi to be united because that will bring so much joy
to his heart. Like a parent who delights in their children
getting along, so God's heart is filled with joy when his
children are united.

The enemy comes to steal, kill, and destroy. He always comes
to divide. Harboring bitterness and resentment for another
person plays into Satan's plan to weaken teams and kill the love
and joy God intends for his people. So we must pray for unity
among our missionaries.

One missionary shared that his team experienced intense op-
position one year. Four missionary families were on this team
for the previous ten years in an African country. A young and
outgoing couple was joining the team, and they quickly became
the talk of the town. The wife had a special lasagna recipe that
the other missionaries loved. Many of the locals were invited
over for meals, and they also enjoyed the new couple's cooking.
The wife was funny and caring, and the husband was witty and
filled with knowledge.

Soon the other missionary wives started to get jealous of their
new friend who had become so popular. Everything she did
became annoying. They also resented her lasagna.

"It's not that great," the other wives would say.

"You know, last time I ate it, I think I got food poisoning."

Somehow, their resentment became centered on her lasagna!
But when one of the families went to the United States for a
furlough, they were able to see how childish and foolish their
attitude had become.

"What in the world are we doing?" they asked. This detached family was able to see more clearly how they had let small things turn into big things. More than that, they were able to see how the enemy was using their own insecurities and pride to divide the team.

That's often how the enemy works in us too. Small things become big things. But when we're in the midst of it, we fall into this trap and let the enemy divide our group. We let the gossip, the jealousy, and even the lasagna become a barrier to unity.

God and Satan both know the power of a united group, a united church. This is why the enemy seeks to divide us. A divided church is the devil's playground.

God loves unity: "Behold, how good and pleasant it is / when brothers dwell in unity!" (Psalm 133:1). God loves to see his children united in heart and purpose for his kingdom.

A friend recently posted a picture on Facebook of his three kids working together on a puzzle. In his post he said, "I need to show this as proof that on this date in history, my kids are not fighting." It may be rare at times, but whenever unity exists, it is beautiful.

My sister and I fought all the time growing up, so when I see siblings getting along well, it always surprises me. When I first met my friend Sean and his sister Tammy, I thought they were boyfriend and girlfriend because of how well they got along and how caring they were toward each other. Sean even said, "We love hanging out together."

I responded with a huge "What?"

So rare—so beautiful.

It's so precious to God that Jesus even prayed for our unity in his great prayer before he was crucified: "I do not ask for these only, but also for those who will believe in me through their word, that they may all be one, just as you, Father, are in me, and I in you, that they also may be in us, so that the world may believe that you have sent me" (John 17:20-21). Our unity delights God, brings power, and serves as a witness to a watching world. The world will know that we are his disciples by the way we love each another, as Jesus tells us in John 13:35. So pray fervently for unity within our missionary teams.

How will unity happen?

PRAY FOR HUMILITY WITHIN THEIR HEARTS

This kind of unity will happen through hearts that are humble toward one another. The main reason for division in any relationship is pride. The main reason for reconciliation is humility.

> *The main reason for division in any relationship is pride. The main reason for reconciliation is humility.*

So if we're praying for unity, it also means we need to pray for humility. Paul says, "Do nothing from selfish ambition or conceit, but in humility count others more significant than yourselves" (Philippians 2:3). Unity happens when we think of others before ourselves. Genuine unity occurs when we value others above ourselves.

I like reading sports biographies. I recently read the story of Phil Jackson, who was an NBA player with the New York Knicks and also coached the Chicago Bulls and Los Angeles Lakers to multiple championships. Jackson said that one of the biggest differences in NBA teams today versus back when he played is the attitude of the players. The hardest part of coaching today's players, he said, is to persuade these athletes to play for the team instead of for themselves.

It's hard for a young man not to put himself first in this age of social media, million-dollar shoe deals, and having his face on posters and magazine covers. Jackson said that when he played, it was about *we*, but now it's about *me*.

But this attitude isn't found only in professional sports. Sadly, it is found in the church too. Instead of thinking of what's best for the church or the ministry, our generation is concerned about what's in it for them. Therefore, it takes humility to say, "I'll live my life for Jesus and others." It takes humility to govern our lives, priorities, and finances by a heart that seeks first God's kingdom rather than our own. It takes humility and courage to say "I'm sorry" and mean it.

One marriage counselor said, "So many marriages could've been saved if just one spouse had the courage to say 'I'm sorry.'" I think it's true not just for marriages but for all relationships: friendships, partnerships, siblings, parents and children, churches, missionaries. So many divisions could have been saved with the simple words "I'm sorry" and "forgive me."

Without a doubt one of the main reasons people leave the mission field is because of strained relationships with other team members. One of my friends said, "Eddie, after being on the mission field for over twenty years, I realize there are a lot of weirdos out there!"

I responded, "Dude, same with expats anywhere!" Sometimes people go to another country because they feel they don't fit in with their home countries. Others go abroad because they are running away from difficult situations or a bad relationship.

But as I was talking to my friend, we both asked, "Wait, do you think other people think that *we're* weird?" We laughed. Deep down, I think we realized we're both pretty different too.

The good news is that God uses the weirdos, the misfits, and the outcasts of this world to do many things that will bring him glory. He uses the foolish things of the world to shame the wise. He uses the weak things of this world to shame the strong. He uses the weirdoes of the world to shame those who think they're normal. Bottom line: it takes humility to attain unity. Without humility we will never have unity. So if we can't see unity in a group, it's probably because humility is missing.

I love what Mother Teresa said about humility: "If we were humble, nothing would change us—neither praise nor discouragement. If someone were to criticize us, we would not feel discouraged. If someone would praise us, we would not feel proud."[1]

Peter reminds us in 1 Peter 5:5: "You who are younger, be subject to the elders. Clothe yourselves, all of you, with humility toward one another, for 'God opposes the proud but gives grace to the humble."' Pray for unity and humility in our hearts and on the mission field.

PRAY FOR DIVINE LOVE FOR ONE ANOTHER

Finally, putting all of these together, we must pray for divine love for one another. We talked about the importance of being connected to Christ in order to love others, but why is loving one another so important in the church and for the mission field? Because ministry is all about relationships. It's not about accomplishing a goal or finishing a task. It's all about relationships.

All of ministry *is* relationship! Loving God and loving our neighbors is all about relationships. "Let each of you look not only to his own interests, but also to the interests of others" (Philippians 2:4). Maturity is when you no longer think only about yourself. That's what children do. Maturity is when you give up thoughts of yourself in order to serve, bless, and love another. And this is crucial for the mission field because Jesus tells us that our love for each other serves as a testimony to our God. Jesus says, "A new commandment I give to you, that you love one another: just as I have loved you, you also are to love one another. By this all people will know that you are my disciples, if you have love for one another" (John 13:34-35).

As one sinner trying to love another sinner, we will quickly discover that we cannot do this on our own power. Our sinful

> *Ministry is all about relationships.*

nature will not allow us to love the one who hurt us or sinned against us. It takes divine grace, divine power, and divine love to love another sinner. And this connects us back to the first point of this chapter: we need to be closely connected to Jesus. In John 15:5 Jesus says that he is the vine and we are his branches. Apart from Jesus, we can do nothing. We can't love apart from Jesus. We can't forgive apart from him.

A missionary couple shared something strange God did as they served the poor and homeless in Seoul, South Korea. The homeless are not easy to be with. Often there are strong odors because the homeless do not shower for months at a time. So the first time this couple served the homeless, the husband confessed that he would often hold his breath. This smell became one of the most challenging parts of their ministry in the early days.

But something happened one day. God gave this couple a love for even the smell of homeless people! They couldn't go a day without smelling the people God called them to love and feed. One time they were given a holiday to get away for a few days by one of the churches that supported them. Those few days apart from those the couple served were difficult. In fact, during those days they actually missed the smell!

God did not give them a new nose; he gave them a new heart. God gave them a divine heart with divine love to be able to fully love the people he had called them to love. We must pray for this heart change to happen to all of our missionaries.

DISCUSSION QUESTIONS

- Share a time when you experienced strong unity within a team or group setting. What were some factors that made the team work so well?

- Do you agree with the statement "Ministry is all about relationships"? Why or why not?

- Why do you think we sometimes allow small things to come between team unity in our churches? What can we do when we see this happening?

PRAYER POINTS

- Pray for your missionaries to experience a closer walk with Jesus today.

- Pray for strong unity within the missionaries' teams. Pray against jealousy and divisions.

- Pray that God would keep their hearts humble and ready to quickly forgive and seek forgiveness when wrongs occur within relationships.

ACTION PLAN

- Are there broken relationships within your own life that need to be mended? Pray for wisdom, grace, humility, and strength to take steps in restoring those relationships.

- Do you know of people whose friendships may have soured because of an unfortunate event between them? Prayerfully and humbly seek ways to be a peacemaker to mediate reconciliation in those relationships.

- As a small group, consider sending a missionary books or resources on relationships or peacemaking.

7

Pray for Never-Ending Devotion

MATTHEW 24:13

WHAT WERE YOU INTO WHEN YOU WERE YOUNGER? Depending on your age, perhaps you were into Beanie Babies. Or if you're a bit older maybe Cabbage Patch Kids were your favorite. My elementary school years were marked by a widespread passion for Pac-Man and Rubik's Cube. The Christmas season often amplifies toy fads. It shocked me to see on the evening news parents fighting over things like Tickle Me Elmo.

Certain fads draw our devotion for a period of time. Whether for a few months or a few years, things like sports, hobbies, or even our careers take a bulk of our time, energy, and passion. Sometimes our church involvement also falls into that category. I hear some people say, "I used to be into church when I was in high school." Or "I used to serve a lot when I was young, but I don't have time for that anymore."

But Jesus was never meant to be a passing fad in our lives. True discipleship with Jesus means he is worthy of our affection, attention, and devotion all the days of our lives. Unfortunately, we can lose this devotion, so we must be careful to keep that flame burning. The enemy wants to snuff it out, so we must be on guard. We must pray for never-ending devotion to Jesus, which we must pray for our missionaries as well.

As we go through the seasons of our lives, different things will demand more of our attention. Parents of young children will focus much more time, resources, and energy on the care of their children. Empty-nesters have a different set of priorities. The same is true for missionaries. Regardless of what season we are in, Jesus requires hearts that are fully his.

How can we pray effectively for this?

PRAY FOR CONVICTION TO DO GOD'S WILL

The first thing we can pray for is conviction in the hearts of missionaries to do God's will. The path we walk begins with our heart's desire. As Jesus was speaking with the Samaritan woman at the well, his disciples urged him to eat something. But he replied, "My food is to do the will of him who sent me and to accomplish his work" (John 4:34). Jesus desired much more than food.

Do we have the same desire? Do we have the conviction that says, "God, I just want to do your will"? This is the heart of someone who has Jesus as their first love, which is not easy to maintain. In fact, as we get older, it gets harder because our hearts can get colder.

I realize that in our discipleship, we not only need to surrender daily but also to have seasons of surrender. When I was in high school, I desperately wanted to appear cool to my peers. That's a huge challenge for high schoolers! However, I knew this was not a priority for God. So I went through a season of surrender in high school. On the cover of all my folders and books, I wrote Romans 1:16—"I am not ashamed of the gospel, for it is the power of God for salvation to everyone who believes"— and other verses to encourage my faith as I struggled with peer pressure.

Then in college, I needed to surrender my desire to make a ton of money and instead offer my future career to the Lord. Seminary was a season of surrender related to my singleness. I felt led to give God my years in seminary and not pursue a relationship with any woman until after graduation. I had to surrender my heart time and again to make sure my desire for a girlfriend didn't overtake my desire for God.

But my surrender didn't stop there. Marriage is another season of surrender as I trusted God and his timing for children (or possibly no children). Parenting is one season after another of surrendering children to the Lord and trusting God to protect and provide for them at the right time. And senior adults offer prayers of surrender, saying, "God, I surrender my golden years into your hands. I don't want to waste them." (Retirement isn't a break from living for God.) It may also mean surrendering our fears of growing older or even of dying.

Every season of our lives brings a new season of surrender to God. There will be new fears, new worries, new temptations, and new opportunities. Faith is a battle of wills. Will we do what *we* want or what *God* wants us to do? It's not an easy fight, which is why so few finish well. As we get older, it gets harder.

Missionaries also face this fight of faith. One missionary in Thailand started off with great passion for the lost. He gave up everything to reach the unreached in the country. He planted churches, started schools, and cared for the poor. Everything was for Christ and his kingdom. But as the years went on and things got harder, his desire for a comfortable life was a growing temptation. Because the dollar goes a long way in Thailand, he wanted to live in a bigger house in a gated community (where the wealthy lived). He hired more domestic helpers. Earlier he hired help to provide needed employment and to evangelize the helpers, but now it was for comfort and show. He said it happened subtly: his heart's desire went from wanting to do God's will to wanting to sit back and live comfortably. So we pray for conviction among our missionaries to do God's will and for never-ending devotion.

Jesus says in Matthew 7:26, "Everyone who hears these words of mine and does not do them will be like a foolish man who built his house on the sand." To hear and not do is foolishness in God's kingdom. To hear and do, having a life that desires to do his will, is wisdom. Therefore, we pray like Jesus, "Not my will, but yours, be done" and "your kingdom come, your will be done, on earth [in my life] as it is in heaven." These are prayers of conviction to do his will.

PRAY FOR COURAGE TO OBEY

Another thing to pray for concerning never-ending devotion is for courage to obey. It's one thing to desire to do God's will, but it's quite another to have the courage to actually obey. In the book of Acts, Peter and the other disciples were jailed and persecuted for preaching Christ, and they were told specifically to stop preaching the gospel message: "We gave you strict orders not to teach in this name," the high priest said. "Yet you have filled Jerusalem with your teaching and are determined to make us guilty of this man's blood." But Peter and the apostles answered, "We must obey God rather than human beings!" (Acts 5:28-29 NIV).

We must obey God rather than human beings!

That takes courage! That takes courage to live out. Just as in the apostles' day, we need men and women, boys and girls, who will proclaim and live the gospel in our day. We need courageous people who will defend and protect the unborn. We need courageous people who will speak truth about God's sacred plan for marriage. We need courageous people who will speak forth truth that Jesus Christ is the only one who can forgive sins and grant life eternal. We need people of courage who say, "We must obey God rather than humans." It takes courage to obey.

Liz was wrestling with going to the Middle East. She had a heart for that part of the world. She saved money to go. She had a strong prayer group supporting her. Everything was set, but she still hesitated. Liz asked me for my advice, and I told her,

"Go for it! Your life will never be the same." She went. And she never was the same. Her heart for the lost and for that part of the world grew.

Be courageous and obey. A life of obedience is what discipleship looks like. The apostle John tells us, "Whoever believes in the Son has eternal life; whoever does not obey the Son shall not see life, but the wrath of God remains on him" (John 3:36). John causally shifts from the word *believe* to the word *obey*. Why? Because those who truly believe will fully obey. First John 5:2 says, "By this we know that we love the children of God, when we love God and obey his commandments." A sign that we are his children is that we love God and obey his commandments. Children of God obey God.

Derek Carr is the quarterback for the Oakland Raiders. He's also a strong believer. He shared recently how he and his brother were giving testimonies at a church conference. After their time of sharing, the pastor gave an altar call and about fifty or sixty people came to the front of the sanctuary to give their lives to Christ. Derek was enjoying what God was doing when suddenly he felt a message from God: "Someone in the crowd is going to attempt suicide tonight. I want you to go back up and pray for him." Derek was nervous. He thought, *What if no one comes up! I'll look like a fool!* But he obeyed. He told the pastor he had something else to share. Then Derek said, "I feel God saying someone here wants to end their life today, but God wants you to know that he loves you, I love you, and God has a wonderful plan for your life. If that's you, I want to pray for you."

As he said this, one guy in the front, eyes filled with tears, pointed to himself, letting Derek know he was speaking to him. They talked late into the night, and Derek shared God's love with the man.

Because of Derek's courageous step to obey, the man's life was saved. God calls us to obey because he wants to bless us and others through us. The path of obedience is always the path of blessing, while disobedience always brings disappointment. God asks us to take steps of faith so he can bless us in ways that we would not have experienced without obeying him. Do you believe this? If you believe, you'll obey.

As the hymn says,

> Trust and obey,
> For there's no other way,
> To be happy in Jesus.
> But to trust and obey.[1]

Let's pray for this kind of courage, faith, and obedience in the hearts of our missionaries and in our hearts as well.

PRAY FOR CONSISTENCY TO PERSEVERE

Concerning never-ending devotion to the Lord, there's one more important item to pray for: consistency to persevere. Jesus reminds us, "The one who endures to the end will be saved" (Matthew 24:13). This speaks to the principle of the perseverance of the saints; those who are truly saved will stay true to the faith to the end. Jesus also says, "Do not work for the food that perishes, but for the food that endures to eternal life, which the Son of Man will give to you. For on him God the Father has set his seal" (John 6:27). The food we eat through a life of faith and obedience results in an enduring faith. But this, of course, does not exclude hard times. We persevere when circumstances are hard. Like Nelson Mandela, who spent twenty-seven years confined to a small prison cell; the floor was his bed and a bucket was his toilet. He was forced to do hard labor and was allowed one visitor per year for just thirty minutes. He endured those years, those days, those minutes, those seconds. Each moment was hard. And we too are to endure. Jesus is saying those who endure hard seasons with faith till the end will be saved.

Does it mean we will never fail or fall? No. But discipleship is not about perfection but direction. We will have our ups and downs in our Christian walk, but we want to keep going one step closer to Christ. Paul reminds us, "Love bears all things, believes all things, hopes all things, endures all things" (1 Corinthians 13:7). True love endures for the sake of the beloved.

When we love our children, we endure their tantrums, their selfishness, their sick days, their potty training days. When we love someone, we endure all things for them. In sickness and in health, for better or for worse. Why? Because that is God's love to us. And that is how we are to love others. Those who truly love God will endure all things as we hold on to God. We love him and trust him.

Within the past year I read two amazing stories. One was of an eighty-year-old grandmother who graduated from college at the same time as her two grandchildren! And another woman named Doreetha Daniels graduated from college at the age of ninety-nine! She lived through the Great Depression, World War II, the civil rights movement, and the moon landing. She also had many personal challenges along the way before graduating. She went through a couple of strokes, she had persistent hearing problems, and she lost some of her eyesight. Because of her age, she also had to give up her driver's license. But at every setback, she got back up.

I love these stories because they illustrate what our life of faith should look like in the end. Success isn't about never having problems or obstacles. Rather, it means overcoming them. Perseverance doesn't mean we never stop but that we start again. When we fall, we crawl to the feet Jesus once again. It means we keep crawling, keep fighting, keep praying, keep reading, keep going back to the cross. That is a picture of never-ending devotion. That is a picture of our life of faith. And that is how I hope our lives and the lives our missionaries will end—with never-ending devotion to Jesus.

DISCUSSION QUESTIONS

- Share some things you particularly enjoyed while growing up. What were the big fads of your childhood? How long did those fads last?

- What are some things you do to help keep the flame and passion of serving Jesus alive in your heart?

- What in your life has required (or requires) much courage? Do you think there's a vacuum of courage in our generation? Why or why not?

PRAYER POINTS

- Ask God to increase your missionaries' desire to do God's will above anyone else's.

- Pray for boldness and courage to obey all that God asks of your missionaries.

- Pray for divine strength for them to persevere.

ACTION PLAN

- Sometimes our passion for God can decrease when we allow idols to creep into our hearts. Ask the Holy Spirit to examine your heart and reveal any idols that need to be surrendered at the foot of the cross.

- What is one thing you've been avoiding that you know God wants you to do (for example, share the gospel with someone or go back to school and finish a degree)? Ask

God to give you courage and begin taking steps to obey today.

- Share with your small group something that you need to persevere in, and ask them to keep you accountable in the months ahead.

8

Pray for Successful Ministry in the Eyes of God

2 TIMOTHY 4:7-8

THIS PAST YEAR was my twenty-fifth high school reunion. Crazy! And yes, I'm old. Since I was living in South Korea, I wasn't able to go to the reunion. Facebook, though, has changed reunions in many ways. Those who attend can look forward to them more because they're already connected to old friends. Reunions used to be a time to see how classmates have changed or how successful they have been. However, reunions aren't the same because we already know how old friends are doing through social media.

As believers, it's important to ask ourselves how we determine success. Do we determine success by judging who's famous? Who's rich? Who still has hair? Success according to the world isn't the same as success in the eyes of God. The value system of God's kingdom is not like this world's. And if we're not careful, we can easily fall into the same trap the rest of the world falls into when thinking about success. It's not about who is most famous or most wealthy. The factors behind success are far more significant than that.

It's okay to want to be successful. I think we should actually strive to be successful. But we need to know the right standard by which to measure success. We want to pray that our missionaries would experience successful lives in the eyes of God.

What does a successful ministry look like to God? How can our missionaries achieve this?

PRAY FOR FOCUS

We must pray that missionaries would have focused lives. To be successful in the eyes of God, we must learn to keep our focus on the race God calls *us* to run. Before Jesus returned to heaven, he told Peter the kind of difficult death he would face. But Peter looked at John and said, "Jesus, what about him?" The Gospel of John says,

> Peter turned and saw the disciple whom Jesus loved following them, the one who also had leaned back against him during the supper and had said, "Lord, who is it that is going to betray you?" When Peter saw him, he said to Jesus, "Lord, what about this man?" Jesus said to him, "If it is my will that he remain until I come, what is that to you? You follow me!" (John 21:20-22)

In essence Jesus says, "It doesn't matter how John's race will finish, Peter; you need to focus on your race!" Jesus is saying to us, "Don't compare your life with someone else's life. Don't compare your suffering with someone else's suffering!"

The enemy commonly tries to make us lose our focus and purpose by comparing our lives with others. When we keep looking at someone else's path, we easily wander off ours. Social media can be a blessing but also a curse. A study done in Denmark found people who stopped using Facebook actually became happier![1] Over one thousand Danes participated in this study; 94 percent of them used Facebook daily. One group continued to use it as usual. The other group stopped using it for a week. Those who stopped using Facebook became happier. The study discovered that social media has a way of making us think that everyone has a better, happier, more successful life than we do. We see their Facebook highlights as if they portray their regular lives. While we're home alone on the computer, we see other's good meals, laughing faces, and vacations on the beach. And all these great moments are happening without us! We're missing out on all the fun. So we begin thinking, *My life is so boring compared to theirs.* That can be depressing. And it actually is for some.

So we learn that one of the easiest ways to make our life miserable is by comparing it to others. We lose gratitude and develop a bad attitude.

This is a difficult experience for me living as an expat for so many years. And it's hard for missionaries too as they see what they're missing. That is why Jesus reminds Peter to keep his focus on his own life. God has a unique path and a unique plan for each of us. The way God will use me will be different from how God will use my friend.

When I first started Crossway Mission Church in 2016, it was challenging. During the first few months, there were many days when I wanted to quit. Wondering *What in the world have I done?* I started looking at other ministries. I thought about other opportunities I had back in the United States, and I also kept looking back to previous ministries (both in South Korea and Australia). *What would things have been like had I stayed longer?* In short, it was making me pretty miserable. Then one day, God clearly spoke to me, "Eddie, stop looking back! I want to do a new thing in your life and in the church, but also *through* the church. So don't keep looking back. Look forward to what I *will* do."

I really needed to hear that!

From that day I stopped looking back or around and focused once again on the path God had given to me. If you want to finish your race well, you must keep your focus on Jesus and *your* race. There are few people more focused than the apostle Paul was, and his words in Acts 20:24 have become my life verse since high school: "I do not account my life of any value nor as precious to myself, if only I may finish my course and the ministry that I received from the Lord Jesus, to testify to the gospel of the grace of God." His focus was on finishing the course that Jesus laid out for his life. This is what we must pray for ourselves and for our missionaries. Then we will not look at what we've given up for Jesus but at what we've gained in Jesus Christ and in the kingdom that is coming!

PRAY FOR FRUITFULNESS

Fruitfulness is another area to pray for concerning successful ministry in God's eyes. We want to pray for lives that are fruitful to the glory of God. Jesus says, "You did not choose me, but I chose you and appointed you that you should go and bear fruit and that your fruit should abide, so that whatever you ask the Father in my name, he may give it to you" (John 15:16). Jesus *chose* you so you might bear fruit that will last.

We need to pray for the fruit of the Spirit: love, joy, peace, patience, kindness, goodness, faithfulness, gentleness, and self-control, which reflect the character of God. When we bear this fruit, others can pick and eat of it from our lives. In all of our circumstances, God has a purpose. One purpose is to make us more like Jesus. We all know and love Romans 8:28: "We know that for those who love God all things work together for good, for those who are called according to his purpose." This tells us the glorious truth that God is sovereign over all things. We believe, embrace, and celebrate this truth for our lives. But that's not all. He reveals his purpose for all of these events that come into our lives in the next verse: "For those whom he foreknew he also predestined to be conformed to the image of his Son, in order that he might be the firstborn among many brothers." God's aim is to conform us into the image of his Son, Jesus Christ.

One important question that can change our perspective in our days of difficulties is to no longer ask *why* but to ask *what*. Many people, when suffering, ask, "Why God? Why is this happening to me? Why now?" This can make us bitter because we don't always know why.

Instead, we should ask, "What do you want me to learn through this? What are you trying to teach me about you, God? What are you trying to show me about your character? What are you revealing about me? What do you want to change in me through this? What do you want me to learn through this?"

Instead of making us bitter disciples, changing our questions can make us *better* disciples. Moving from *why* to *what* can change our lives and transform our faith. And that will create much more fruit in our lives.

So instead of asking, "*Why* am I still in this job, God?" Ask, "*What* do you want me to learn while in this job? *What* do you want me to see differently?"

Instead of asking, "*Why* am I still single?" Ask, "*What* do you want to mature in me? *What* kind of character do you want to develop in me?"

That one change is the difference between *bitter* and *better*. But this kind of fruit can be developed only from a life of faith that is dependent on Christ. Remember John 15:5: "I am the vine; you are the branches. Whoever abides in me and I in him, he it is that bears much fruit, for apart from me you can do nothing." A life attached to Christ, abiding in Christ, trusting in Christ will bear fruit. So when this kind of fruit is missing from our lives, we need to examine what we are rooted in.

We must pray for this kind of fruitfulness in the lives of missionaries because only through the divine help of the Spirit can they love enemies and desire them to become family. Only through the help of the Spirit can they extend great patience and kindness to those who test their patience.

PRAY FOR FAITHFULNESS

A third way to pray for a successful ministry in the eyes of God is to pray for faithfulness. The words we long to hear when we finish the race are found in Matthew 25:23: "Well done, good and faithful servant. You have been faithful over a little; I will set you over much. Enter into the joy of your master." We are saved by faith but rewarded for faithfulness. Jesus reveals here that small acts of faithfulness will be greatly and generously rewarded in heaven. And all of this is out of the joy of the Father in heaven! Enter into the joy of your Master.

Therefore we must not overlook the importance of being faithful to small things. So we pray for faithfulness in small things. And it's important that we are faithful—even when forgotten.

After my freshman year in college, I went on my first mission trip, which was to Kenya, Africa, with the campus church I was a part of. Each day was filled with ministry and activity—from teaching to evangelism to vacation Bible school to outreach. Each night was a great time to get to know the missionaries. One evening I was talking with Sam, who, with his team, was reaching out to one of the unreached people groups of the hill tribes of Kenya. They were doing some great pioneering work. As he explained the work they were doing, I said, "Great job! You're doing such great work for the kingdom!" He said, "Thanks. But there are a lot of challenges."

When they first came to the mission field, he said it was awesome and he'd loved every minute of it. He had appreciated the care packages, the letters from home, the phone calls, the encouragement. It was all so strengthening.

But after a year or two passed by, Sam said that those calls, letters, and care packages stopped coming, and he began to feel forgotten. Those times were a reality check. *What am I doing this for? Who am I doing this for?* Then Sam said, "It's at those times that you remind yourself, *I'm doing this for God, and God alone.*"

Another missionary shared how difficult it was to visit their sending churches every six years because instead of feeling like he had come home, he felt like a stranger. Missionaries often don't recognize people and no one recognizes them.

So it's utterly important to honor and care for our missionaries but also to pray that all of us would remain faithful to the Lord, even when forgotten. We must remember that though we may be forgotten by others, we are never forgotten by God!

A good friend of mine dreamed of being a missionary in the Muslim world. I met Alex during a

> *We must remember that though we may be forgotten by others, we are never forgotten by God!*

trip to Morocco. She was in her thirties and single. But Alex said God delayed her move to the Middle East by five years, and she almost thought she wouldn't make it there. She gave her life to missions in college and told God, "Here I am! Send me!" She got connected with a mission agency after college and expected to go on the field within that year.

But her visa got delayed by more than a year. So during that time Alex helped in the office of the mission agency. Though she didn't know much about computers, she studied and learned and was able to help them set up the internet network.

Then there was another delay. Alex waited a second year, during which she helped with audio equipment to record and produce mission radio broadcasts. Then she learned about fixing cars. All this time Alex cried out in prayer, *God! Why all these delays? Why all this waiting? I'm ready to go now! I'm ready to reach the Muslim world!*

But God kept delaying her departure to the Middle East, simply saying to her, "Wait. And be faithful in the small things." Then, during another year of waiting, Alex learned how to sew her own clothes. Only after a five-year delay did God finally open the door for her to go.

Alex went and lived in a rural and unreached area. Her office had no internet, so her experience of setting up networks came in handy. And because her area didn't have many TVs, many people listened to the radio, so she started developing radio programs with the gospel message for her community. Then her car broke down, but her knowledge of car repair came in handy. And thanks to her sewing lessons, she was not only able to make her own clothes but also new clothes for the poorer children in her community. Alex realized that those five years of waiting weren't wasted. It was a time of preparation!

In each area of her life, Alex was being faithful in the small things God had asked her to do. She thought these were menial tasks, but they were God's way of preparing her for bigger things later on. Faithfulness in small things prepared her for the bigger roles God wanted to bring into her life. God never wastes time. Every season of waiting is a season of preparing. So be faithful now. Be faithful in small things. Be faithful in hidden things. God is preparing us for greater things!

So don't sulk and ask, *Why is this happening?* Ask instead, *What do you want me to learn, God? How do you want me to change? How can I trust you more through this?* God is preparing us for our next season and next assignment. And that new season's arrival will be connected to how well we prepare by being faithful in today's small things. This is a successful life in the eyes of God.

> *God never wastes time. Every season of waiting is a season of preparing.*

It is so important that we do it all for Jesus. Big things, small things, hidden things. Through it all, we keep our eyes on him. We are to focus on him and the race that he calls us to run. Then we can have the confidence to say at the end of our race,

> I have fought the good fight, I have finished the race, I have kept the faith. Henceforth there is laid up for me the crown of righteousness, which the Lord, the righteous judge, will award to me on that day, and not only to me but also to all who have loved his appearing. (2 Timothy 4:7-8)

Great reward awaits those who finish their race and long for his return. That is success in the eyes of heaven. When we finish our races, may we and our missionaries be found successful in the eyes of God.

DISCUSSION QUESTIONS

- Has your definition of *success* changed over the years? If so, how?

- Why do you think we so easily compare our race with those of others? What can we do to help keep our eyes on our own race?

- When you think of faithfulness, who do you think of? Share why they come to mind.

PRAYER POINTS

- Ask God to help keep the eyes of our missionaries focused on Jesus and on the race God has called each of them to run. Pray that they won't compare their journey with others.

- Ask that God would make their lives abundantly fruitful— with the fruit of the Spirit—for the kingdom.

- Pray that God would keep our missionaries faithful till the end.

ACTION PLAN

- Write on a piece of paper what you believe success is from God's perspective for your life, family, work, and ministry. If you're married, have your spouse also do this and compare your lists.

- What do you want your epitaph to say? Write one or two sentences of what you hope it will say.

- In the discussion questions, you were asked to think of someone who is faithful. If possible, contact that person this week and let them know you think of them as a particularly faithful person.

9

Pray for Churches to Partner Well

PHILIPPIANS 4:10-20

MINISTRY CAN OFTEN BE LONELY, and the mission field can feel even lonelier. Whether they pastor a small or a large church, many pastors feel alone. And my discussions with many missionaries has confirmed they feel lonely to an even greater degree. This is because missionaries are separated not just from community but from their own culture and other forms of comfort. But when churches support them well, it makes a huge difference in their lives. A good partnership between a church and a missionary gives strength, brings life, and increases the missionary's energy for the task ahead. But a weak partnership often makes a missionary feel all alone. So we need to pray for strong partnerships to exist between missionaries and the churches that support them.

PRAY FOR CHURCHES TO BE SENDERS

How can we pray for churches to partner well with their missionaries on the field? We begin by praying for churches to actively and consistently send people to the mission field. And this requires churches to be committed to the Great Commission as a core value. I've heard many pastors say, "A great commitment to the Great Commission will build a great church!" I believe that is true.

Jesus' call to make disciples, baptize them, and teach them (Matthew 28:18-20) is clear for all churches and all believers. We are to be committed to finishing the Great Commission with all the resources we have.

Regarding our role in missions, John Piper often says we have only three options: Go. Send. Or disobey. We go to the peoples and places that do not know Jesus. And if God has called an individual to stay, then they support well and send out those who go! Now I intentionally said, "If God has called an individual to *stay*" because many people wait for God to call them to go, but he already has! The default status is to go! Kingdom culture in a church is a sending culture to the nations.

Jesus said to his disciples, "The harvest is plentiful, but the laborers are few; therefore pray earnestly to the Lord of the harvest to send out laborers into his harvest" (Matthew 9:37-38). So churches must pray that God would send out workers into *his* harvest fields. Pray that God would send out workers through *your* church. Churches must have a culture of people going and ready to go when God calls.

Serving in an expat church in South Korea has its challenges, but I love that everyone here has already taken the big step of leaving the familiar comforts of home and has adjusted to a new life in a new culture and a new country. That's not easy to do.

I often challenge the expats in our church, when your work contracts expire, don't make going back to your home country your default option. Ask God for a nation to be sent to. You can still do your regular vocation as a teacher, counselor, lawyer, or doctor. But now do that work in a nation that needs more of a Christian witness. I have been greatly blessed to see the shift in our church's culture, with many of our members leaving South Korea for places like the Middle East, Southeast Asia, and even Europe. I've been impressed by the steps of faith taken by these church members as they go to new countries, and they have seen growth in their spiritual lives as a result.

To make this a part of a church's culture, they need to preach and teach on missions regularly. Churches are to be sending bodies to the nations. Rick Warren says, "You don't judge a church by its seating capacity but its sending capacity."[1] So often we focus on how many are gathering or sitting in our sanctuaries. But we also need to ask, "How many are we sending out?" and then pray that churches are significant senders through their ministries. And when God calls us to stay, we give our money and pray.

Saddleback Church of Lake Forest, California, is the first church to send out mission teams (long-term and short-term) to every country in the world. That is amazing! And it took a lot of intentional planning. They have strategically made sure they are sending people to places in need of the gospel. They have created a culture in which people are expected to be involved in missions as a regular part of their discipleship.

That's what normal Christian discipleship is supposed to look like: loving Jesus and loving what Jesus loves. And he loves the lost. He loves the nations. So our churches should be marked by that kind of love too.

Pray for strong churches that send missionaries.

PRAY FOR CHURCHES TO BE SUPPORTERS

We must pray for churches to be regular and consistent supporters of their missionaries. Not only do we want a culture of sending in our churches, we also want a culture of generous support. Paul says, "Let the elders who rule well be considered worthy of double honor, especially those who labor in preaching and teaching" (1 Timothy 5:17). Timothy needs to set up the leadership culture of the church Paul planted in Ephesus. And a primary role for the church is to take care of their preachers, teachers, and pastors (and I believe missionaries fall under that as well).

Honor leaders, but those who labor and work through preaching and teaching are worthy of double honor, meaning extra care and support. Paul is speaking of financial provisions. He goes on, "For the Scripture says, 'You shall not muzzle an ox when it treads out the grain,' and, 'The laborer deserves his wages'" (1 Timothy 5:18). Those who work for the church deserve adequate compensation from the church. In other words, be sure to feed those who lead.

One professor and pastor I know shared about how he was asked to be the guest speaker at a church retreat. This retreat center was about a three-hour drive for him—that's a lot of time and a lot of gas. He preached for four days, several times each day. And at the end of the retreat, the leader of the group called him up and said, "Everyone give our speaker a hand!" (They clapped.) "And to express our appreciation for coming to speak at our retreat, we want to give you this as a thank you gift for serving us!"

And they gave him their church T-shirt. That's it. No honorarium. No gas money. That was it. A T-shirt! This particular professor wrote a blog about his experience and was shocked and saddened to find that many other pastors had similar experiences. One pastor replied to him, "At least you got something!" After this person's speaking engagement, all he got was applause!

It was so sad to see how these churches viewed their speakers but also their guests. Let's pray for a generous culture to be created in our churches. And in a similar way, we need to pray that churches and Christians would be faithful, generous supporters of missionaries through their financial giving as well.

Look at how Paul remembers the support he received for his missions work from the church in Philippi:

It was kind of you to share my trouble. And you Philippians yourselves know that in the beginning of the gospel, when I left Macedonia, no church entered into partnership with me in giving and receiving, except you only. Even in

Thessalonica you sent me help for my needs once and again.
(Philippians 4:14-16)

He's thanking this church because, for a while, no one supported
him except the church in Philippi. They supported willingly, sac-
rificially, and generously.

Henry became wealthy from his business while in his early
thirties. He wasn't making millions but tens of millions of dollars
each year. Initially, he did what a lot of young people do. He
bought more cars, a bigger house, and traveled first class. But one
day Nate, a fellow Christian in business who was much older and
wiser, challenged Henry not with words but with his lifestyle.
Nate also made a lot of money over the years, but he determined
how much he needed to live and then gave away the rest. So Nate
was practicing a reverse tithe. Instead of giving 10 percent and
keeping 90 percent, he kept 10 percent and gave away 90 percent.
Henry was challenged by Nate's generosity and began committing
to give more of his finances back to God as well. Henry was
learning an important spiritual principle concerning wealth and
faith: God increases our wealth not so we can increase our standard
of living but so we can increase our standard of giving. Now, obvi-
ously most of us couldn't live off of 10 percent of what we make,
but we want to cultivate in our lives the principle of generosity.

I know other families who committed to increasing their
giving by a half percent or a quarter percent each year to the
church and to missions work. We should prayerfully challenge
ourselves to consider this. Paul says to the Philippians,

Not that I seek the gift, but I seek the fruit that increases to your credit. I have received full payment, and more. I am well supplied, having received from Epaphroditus the gifts you sent, a fragrant offering, a sacrifice acceptable and pleasing to God. And my God will supply every need of yours according to his riches in glory in Christ Jesus. To our God and Father be glory forever and ever. Amen. (Philippians 4:17-20)

Paul is reminding them that their giving is never a waste. This isn't prosperity preaching. He's not saying, "Give to God and you'll get a new car or bigger house!" He's saying that our giving has spiritual and eternal significance in the eyes of God! The Lord will bless us in ways we can never imagine, be it here on earth or in eternity. And we want to pray that this kind of support and giving would also be poured into missions work to the unreached and unengaged parts of the world.

What's sad is less than 5 percent of all money given to missions is used for the least-reached places of the world. That is why our church supports the Lausanne Movement and other missions that are intentionally focused on finishing the Great Commission by going to unreached parts of the world. Therefore, pray for strong churches that are active and generous supporters of missions.

PRAY FOR CHURCHES TO BE SHELTERS

We also must pray that churches would be shelters for their missionaries. Paul says to the Philippian church, "I rejoiced in the

Lord greatly that now at length you have revived your concern for me. You were indeed concerned for me, but you had no opportunity" (Philippians 4:10). At the heart of this message is a plea that our churches would care about the well-being of our missionaries. It's too easy to give money but not think further about missions work. It's too easy for things to be out of sight and therefore out of mind.

Partnering well in missions means we create a church culture in which we shelter our missionaries in prayer. Paul says to the church at Colossae,

> Epaphras, who is one of you, a servant of Christ Jesus, greets you, always struggling on your behalf in his prayers, that you may stand mature and fully assured in all the will of God. For I bear him witness that he has worked hard for you and for those in Laodicea and in Hierapolis. (Colossians 4:12-13)

We want our missionaries to know that churches are fighting for them in prayer. So we pray for divine rest, divine energy, divine joy, and divine protection in the lives of our missionaries.

In the early days of my church plant, I made it mandatory for members of our church pray ten minutes each day for the church and its leadership. We can determine the culture we want to create, so I decided to make sure a culture of prayer was there from the beginning. I can testify that I felt a difference in our ministry once our people committed to praying every day. Prayers make a difference.

Because of how God uses prayer and because of how powerful prayers are, the enemy will do all he can do stop us from praying. Don't give in. Keep praying. Fight to get on your knees. Fight to stay on your knees. And then learn to fight on your knees.

I want missionaries to experience this blessing of being covered in prayer. Don't give up praying for them. Instead, pray that intercessory prayer would increase. Pray that churches will be the much-needed partners and supporters for all their missionaries.

DISCUSSION QUESTIONS

- Before reading this chapter, what did you think the role of the local church was in the life of a missionary? Has it changed after reading this? If so, how?

- Do you know how many people from your church have been sent to the mission field (either short-term or long-term)?

- What do think about the statement that we should be concerned about a church's sending capacity, not just its seating capacity?

PRAYER POINTS

- Pray that God will give the global church a deeper understanding of its vital role to send out and support missionaries around the world.

- Pray that God will create a culture in your church that desires and inspires others to go to the nations.

- Pray that your church will be faithful in prayer and generous in giving to your missionaries.

ACTION PLAN

- Find out what your church does to support and encourage your missionaries. See if there are ways you and your small group could help in that support.

- With approval from your church's leadership, consider having prayer campaigns throughout the year with focused seasons of hearing updates from your missionaries and increased opportunities to pray for them.

- If you've never been on a mission trip, prayerfully consider going on one this upcoming year—maybe even as a small group.

10

Pray for Agencies to Partner Well

2 TIMOTHY 3:16-17

I SAW A DOCUMENTARY RECENTLY on Ronald Reagan's presidency during the 1980s. One thing that stood out to me was that even though he served two terms (for eight years), three different sets of teams helped him. For many observers of his presidential leadership, it almost seemed like he had three terms because those in a president's inner circle determine his success. Historians noted how his first team was strong and made a great first impression on the world. The next team had people in the wrong places, and Reagan appeared weak and uncertain during those years. After another shuffle, Reagan's final team not only allowed him to end well, but the momentum led to George H. W. Bush, his vice president, winning the presidency after him. I learned through this documentary that though we mainly see the president, his counsel and inner circle are vital to his success. That kind of partnership is crucial for a leader.

The same can be said of missionaries. Their success is based on the strength of two key partnerships: (1) their supporting churches and (2) their mission agency.

If people forget to pray for their pastors even though they see them once a week, the same is even truer of their missionaries. And even fewer pray for mission agencies. In fact, one person said that he has never heard anyone asking churches to pray for the mission agencies. But they are vital, and we don't want to forget them.

We often think of the church as helping missionaries, but rarely do we think of helping mission agencies. However, if we're going to see the mission of Jesus completed, we also need to pray for the role of mission agencies in the life of our missionaries. Agencies serve an important role in preparing, equipping, and logistics. These aspects of missions are rarely talked about in the church, and therefore we rarely pray about them corporately or individually.

Behind every great missionary is a great church and a great mission agency.

PRAY FOR DISCERNMENT IN SELECTION

How should we pray for mission agencies? We begin by asking God to give these agencies discernment in selecting their missionary candidates. We see the need for discernment in the selection process as the early church selected deacons. The twelve apostles instructed the disciples to

"Pick out from among you seven men of good repute, full of the Spirit and of wisdom, whom we will appoint to this

duty. But we will devote ourselves to prayer and to the
ministry of the word." And what they said pleased
the whole gathering, and they chose Stephen, a man full
of faith and of the Holy Spirit, and Philip, and Prochorus,
and Nicanor, and Timon, and Parmenas, and Nicolaus, a
proselyte of Antioch. These they set before the apostles,
and they prayed and laid their hands on them. (Acts 6:3-6)

We see the importance of the selection process for deacons.
They sought people who had evidence of the Holy Spirit at work
in their life. They looked for people of wisdom and faith. Paul
also lists qualities to look for when picking elders:

An overseer, as God's steward, must be above reproach. He
must not be arrogant or quick-tempered or a drunkard or
violent or greedy for gain, but hospitable, a lover of good,
self-controlled, upright, holy, and disciplined. He must
hold firm to the trustworthy word as taught, so that he may
be able to give instruction in sound doctrine and also to
rebuke those who contradict it. (Titus 1:7-9)

In light of these instructions, we must remember that missionaries are church leaders on the mission field. Some will be the
first church leaders a city or a country has ever had. So it is
crucial for churches and agencies to have great wisdom and
discernment. They need to discern the character, calling, and
compatibility of the mission teams.

Many people who may want to be missionaries may not be
ready or even called to the mission field. Agencies need biblical

discernment to determine whether mission candidates' characters match Scripture. They need to discern whether a candidate is truly called as well. Mission agency leaders informed me that many people want to join a mission for the wrong reasons. Some people have what leaders call "missionary hero syndrome"; they see themselves as a savior, thinking, *Those poor people need me to save them!*

Others think they will be respected by peers for their sacrifice. Part of the selection process is determining whether a candidate will have the compatibility (and humility) to work well in a team setting. "It's better to have no person than the wrong person" is an important principle, but it's often difficult to uphold. Missions agencies, like all organizations, are tempted to plug people into holes rather than waiting for God to provide the right people.

One mission agency was in desperate need of a missionary to go to a risky area in the Middle East. A new recruit seemed a bit too eager to go to that location. There were questions concerning his character and ability to follow orders. But the agency desperately needed someone to go, so despite their initial reservation, they sent this guy. He ended up taking charge, was unable to listen to orders, and disrupted team dynamics. And while hosting a short-term team, instead of following orders and taking several cars so as not to draw attention to the team, he rented a bus so they could all be together. On top of that, while the bus was going through a dangerous area, he decided to blast praise songs through the windows. The attention he drew to the team put them into some dangerous situations with the locals.

This shows the importance of discernment in selecting who will join a team on the mission field. One leader said, "Making a bad team hire is far more costly than most people realize." Having the wrong person can demoralize highly motivated people, become a financial drain, and waste time on projects. In short, it can destroy a team. Conflict within teams is a major reason why people leave the mission field.

It's important for us to pray for mission agencies' discernment in selecting the right people, for the right places, and for the right teams.

PRAY FOR DISCIPLESHIP TRAINING

Discipleship training for mission agencies is another area of prayer we need to focus on. We must pray that after candidates are selected they will be well-trained for the mission field. The apostle Paul says, "All Scripture is breathed out by God and profitable for teaching, for reproof, for correction, and for training in righteousness, that the man of God may be complete, equipped for every good work" (2 Timothy 3:16-17). All training and discipleship must be grounded in the Bible. We must raise up lovers of God's Word. Remember that we are called to be and to make disciples of Jesus. The word *disciple* means "student" or "learner." So, to be disciples of Jesus means we are students of God's Word for all our lives.

Second Timothy reminds us that the Word is breathed by God and useful to train us and equip God's people for every good work. The good work we do for God overflows out of our connection to God's Word. In Luke 9:1-6 we catch a glimpse of how Jesus trained the disciples:

> He called the twelve together and gave them power and authority over all demons and to cure diseases, and he sent them out to proclaim the kingdom of God and to heal. And he said to them, "Take nothing for your journey, no staff, nor bag, nor bread, nor money; and do not have two tunics. And whatever house you enter, stay there, and from there depart. And wherever they do not receive you, when you leave that town shake off the dust from your feet as a testimony against them." And they departed and went through the villages, preaching the gospel and healing everywhere.

Jesus not only taught them God's Word but also gave them his authority. He gave them opportunities to practice what they learned, to preach and to heal in the communities.

Mission agencies prepare their candidates in many ways:

- crosscultural adjustments
- anthropology
- missions strategies
- church planting
- language preparation

The list can go on and on. So let's pray for their training process to be effective. The preparation time is life changing for many candidates. I created a sixteen-week short-term missions training course that I've been using for the past twenty years. The preparation changed many short-termers' lives even before they went on the trip. Many people grew through prayer, Bible memorization, studies in missions, and studies in culture and language. And through these trips people grew spiritually and became leaders within the church.

On the flip side, when we were serving some missionaries in Laos for a short-term trip, the two full-time missionaries saw what we were doing to prepare each day and night and looked at our missions training manual. They confessed that they'd not gone through proper training before being sent to the field. So, during our few weeks together, they joined us for our morning and evening meetings and said it was a wake-up call for them. They saw the importance of preparing before going to the mission field.

If you are praying about going to the mission field, invest your life in the Word of God, in discipleship, and in discipling others. A missionary in Indonesia taught his church to always ask each other, "Who are you discipling, and who is discipling you?" Those are great questions for every local church.

PRAY FOR STRONG PARTNERSHIPS
WITH CHURCHES

Mission agencies need strong partnerships with churches. The enemy will always seek to destroy partnerships in the gospel, so pray that these relationships would be protected and remain strong. In 2 Corinthians 8:23-24 we catch a glimpse of the various partnerships Paul and the churches shared in his missions: "Titus . . . is my partner and fellow worker for your benefit. And as for our brothers, they are messengers of the churches, the glory of Christ. So give proof before the churches of your love and of our boasting about you to these men." Paul says this in the context of giving to and supporting missions work through the church. And we see Paul seeking to honor his partners, the work they are doing, and the other missionaries and messengers who have gone to other cities and churches with the gospel.

Churches and agencies play a role in keeping missionaries accountable, not just with finances but in other areas, such as moral integrity. They also play a key role in helping missionaries prepare for and respond to crises, failures, and even discouragement and depression. As missionaries visit the United States, churches and agencies help them to adjust and transition well back to life in their home church. They also play a key role in helping raise funds and prayer support for the missionary.

So we must pray that the partnership of churches and agencies provides support and strength for our missionaries.

DISCUSSION QUESTIONS

- Before reading this chapter, what was your view of mission agencies and their role within the life of a missionary? How has it developed since reading this chapter?

- What are some unique ways an agency can help prepare a missionary in training that a local church might not be as equipped to do?

- What are ways that you and your church can reach out to and serve mission agencies?

PRAYER POINTS

- Ask God to give mission agencies a greater sense of discernment when selecting missionary candidates.

- Pray for strong discipleship training within the candidate preparation process.

- Pray for a good relationship between agencies and your church in effectively supporting your missionaries.

ACTION PLAN

- Find out which mission agencies are connected to your missionaries and begin praying for them by name. Contact those agencies and ask them for prayer requests and share the requests with your church.

- Ask your church leadership to consider inviting some mission agencies to present the work they do for your congregation.

- If there's a local office or branch of a mission agency connected to your missionary, consider doing a day of service for them (e.g., clean their office) or take the staff out for a meal.

11

Pray for Reentering Well

HEBREWS 12:1-2

REMEMBER WHAT IT WAS LIKE the first time you went home after a long period away? You'll understand this feeling especially if you lived abroad. I remember visiting the United States after living in South Korea for a while. I loved going to Walmart and Target just to see all the items I couldn't buy in South Korea. I wanted to buy everything because it was so inexpensive! And then there were the things I longed to eat: In-N-Out Burger and Chick-fil-A. But as the years away increased, my returns home started to feel different. I no longer felt like I was going home. Instead, I felt like a visitor in a foreign land.

Those chips I used to eat seem so salty now. And were the burritos at Chipotle always this big? Why does everything seem so big, so salty, so different? One of the biggest challenges in coming back is realizing that things have changed, people have changed, and I have changed. Reentry for us can be hard, but reentry for missionaries is even harder.

I know one missionary couple whose hearts break every time they come home. Their adult children give them guilt trips for spending more time with the children in another country than with their own grandchildren in the United States. Coming back to one's home country can be even harder than the first time leaving. This important prayer topic is rarely addressed.

So we want to pray for our missionaries' times of reentry and transition in their home countries.

PRAY THEY WILL BE RECEIVED WELL

Returning to their home country often doesn't feel like they've come home. The church has changed and so have the missionaries. Familiar faces are now gone. So, it's crucial to pray that returning missionaries will be received upon coming home.

This is not just a good idea; it is God's call for the church. Look at Matthew 10:40, where Jesus speaks to his disciples about the blessing that comes to those who receive them well: "Whoever receives you receives me, and whoever receives me receives him who sent me." When we receive the people God has sent, we are receiving Jesus! When we welcome and bless his servants, we are welcoming and blessing him!

Then Jesus says, "The one who receives a prophet because he is a prophet will receive a prophet's reward, and the one who receives a righteous person because he is a righteous person will receive a righteous person's reward" (Matthew 10:41). This is an incredible promise. If you welcome, bless, honor, and host a missionary because they are missionaries (servants of God), you will receive a reward from God as if you were the missionary! That. Is. Amazing.

We don't want to elevate missionaries, pastors, or leaders to the point of idolatry. But we do honor those God desires to honor. I know of one US family who bought a home with an extra bedroom specifically because they wanted to host missionaries or guest speakers in town. I stayed in their home when I was guest speaking for their church near San Francisco. I remember feeling like I was a part of their family. The hospitality they offered was a picture of God's gracious love for the visitor (and even the stranger). It was a beautiful reminder that we who share a common faith in Christ are truly family in Christ.

In Matthew 10:42 Jesus says, "Whoever gives one of these little ones even a cup of cold water because he is a disciple, truly, I say to you, he will by no means lose his reward." Jesus says even small acts of service and love will not go unnoticed by our Father in heaven. The reason he uses this example is to show how even small, seemingly insignificant acts of service matter to God.

How we treat his servants matters to God! Look at what Paul says to the Philippians about Epaphroditus: "Receive him in the Lord with all joy, and honor such men, for he nearly died for the work of Christ, risking his life to complete what was lacking in your service to me" (Philippians 2:29-30). Epaphroditus was sent by the church in Philippi to meet Paul's needs while he was in jail. During this more than thirty-day journey over 730 miles, Epaphroditus became ill and almost died. And for this act of service, Paul says, "Honor him!" And honor people like him, those who give their lives for the gospel. Therefore, pray that churches would love, serve, and receive missionaries well.

PRAY THEY WILL REST WELL

Second, pray that our missionaries' time at home will be restful. When missionaries return home, it can take a lot of time to feel rested again. It's been said that the heavier the burdens, the longer the recovery. If you've been burned out or wiped out, it can take a while before you get back to being yourself. And many missionaries need time to rest.

So, pray through Psalm 23 for their lives. Psalm 23:1-3 says,

> The LORD is my shepherd; I shall not want.
>
> He makes me lie down in green pastures.
> He leads me beside still waters.
>
> He restores my soul.

Jesus, our good Shepherd, sometimes makes us lie down and rest. And in that place of rest, he restores our soul.

In Matthew 11:28-30 Jesus says: "Come to me, all who labor and are heavy laden, and I will give you rest. Take my yoke upon you, and learn from me, for I am gentle and lowly in heart, and you will find rest for your souls. For my yoke is easy, and my burden is light." Only Jesus gives rest to our souls. Only Jesus restores our souls. Because our souls find their rest in God alone. This shows us that there is a rest that we need that sleep cannot give to us. There is a rest that our souls long for that can only be satisfied in the presence of Jesus. True rest comes in his presence. True restoration comes from Christ alone. Pray that when missionaries come home, they will be able to find true rest in him.

Every time I'm on a mission trip, especially in a Muslim country, I cannot get deep sleep. There's a spiritual heaviness in some of those places. The constant fight is draining. I'm tired, but I can't sleep.

One winter, I was driving in Chicago on icy roads. Suddenly the car in front of me braked hard and started spinning around! So I too braked hard and my car did a 360-degree spin. My whole body tensed, bracing for an impact as I saw cars around me spinning too. But I only hit a snow bank. I got out of the car, checking for damage. The car was okay. But when I got home, I was exhausted. Being tense for those few seconds left my body depleted of energy for the rest of the day.

That's what some missionaries go through every day. The tension from culture stress and the weariness from spiritual warfare has a draining effect on the body, mind, and soul.

Many missionaries aren't aware of this tension until they're home for a while. Once they start to unwind, some crash emotionally and physically. So they need our prayers for rest! When you meet a missionary who's taking a break from the mission field, pray that God would grant them physical, emotional, and spiritual rest.

During our church's leadership training, we've been looking at the importance of emotional health in the life of a leader. Peter Scazzero says, "The emotionally unhealthy leader is someone who operates in a continuous state of emotional and spiritual deficit, lacking emotional maturity and a 'being with God' sufficient to sustain their 'doing for God.'"[1]

We learned that when our *doing* for God is more than our *being* with God, there will be a disconnect in our soul. That disconnect will eventually result in decreased joy. And this spiritual deficit reveals itself oftentimes in too much activity. Unhealthy and unrested leaders engage in more activities than their combined spiritual, physical, and emotional reserves can sustain. When we give out for God more than we receive from God, we are running on empty. Many missionaries feel empty by the time they go on sabbatical or return home. Therefore, we must pray they will rest well when they return home.

PRAY THEY WILL READJUST WELL

Third, pray that our missionaries readjust well to their home countries. A big part of readjusting involves processing the challenges they've faced while in a foreign land. Some have to fight depression or bitterness because they feel they've suffered more than they expected. Others battle anxiety; they couldn't wait to go home—until they got there. Then they want to go back to the mission field.

Paul's word of encouragement to them is, "I consider that the sufferings of this present time are not worth comparing with the glory that is to be revealed to us" (Romans 8:18). Whatever difficulties and discomforts we face in this lifetime are nothing compared to the glory we will experience when Christ returns. There will be no comparison. So we must learn to filter our frustrations through this lens of faith. We must see all the frustrating or painful moments of life through the lens of eternity.

When we live like this, a moment of suffering endured with faith in Christ impacts our eternal reward.

A difficulty some missionaries face in reentry is that they no longer feel like their native country is their home. They've been away for so long that they feel like a foreigner. Thus, some missionaries go through reverse culture shock.

These are some of the reverse culture shock moments I've had when I've returned to the United States:

- Wait, people are lining up in a straight line? Where am I?

- What do you mean I can't get everything delivered to my home?

- Why is there so much parking space at this Costco? Is it closed today?

I left the United States in 1995, after graduating from college. Since then I've lived in Canada for three years, South Korea for three years, Australia for seven years, and now South Korea again for nine years. I feel like I don't have a home country anymore. When I'm in America, it feels foreign, and people ask, "Where are you from?" The Australians also asked, "Where are you from?" (Even though I'm an Australian citizen now too. My accent gave it away.) And of course in South Korea, I get asked that too. In fact, I speak Korean in stores, but store workers usually reply in English. I keep speaking in Korean, and they keep speaking in English. The clear message is, "You're not from here." (And your Korean isn't as good as you think!)

In all these things I am reminded that this country is not my home—because this world is not my home. A big part of readjusting is refocusing on Christ and our eternal kingdom with him, which is why Hebrews 12:1-2 is so important to keep in mind.

> Therefore, since we are surrounded by so great a cloud of witnesses, let us also lay aside every weight, and sin which clings so closely, and let us run with endurance the race that is set before us, looking to Jesus, the founder and perfecter of our faith, who for the joy that was set before him endured the cross, despising the shame, and is seated at the right hand of the throne of God.

The only way to readjust well is to refocus our eyes on Jesus. When Jesus is at the center, we are able to keep the main thing the main thing. When we lose focus on Jesus, secondary things become central. Hebrews reminds us to focus on Jesus and realize we aren't surrounded by suffering but by the saints, who are cheering us on: "Keep going! You're almost there! You're almost home!"

Hebrews 11:24-26 says,

> By faith Moses, when he was grown up, refused to be called the son of Pharaoh's daughter, choosing rather to be mistreated with the people of God than to enjoy the fleeting pleasures of sin. He considered the reproach of Christ greater wealth than the treasures of Egypt, for he was looking to the reward.

Moses was able to endure mistreatment because he was looking ahead to his eternal reward. We too can endure as we look ahead. We have hope as we see what is to come. And we can adjust through all seasons of life when we remember we are not yet home. So let's pray this faith will grow in us and in our missionaries. Pray that reentry for them will mean reentering the presence of God and refocusing their lives to be all about him.

Daisy spent thirty-one years as a single missionary teaching Chinese children at a small rural school and discipling many of the women in her village. Many lives were changed because of Daisy's ministry. She and they were blessed. But another blessing was that one of her sending churches in North Carolina prepared for her retirement and return home to the United States. Upon her arrival at the airport, over eighty church members held signs and balloons congratulating her for her time on the mission field. At first she thought a celebrity or famous athlete was coming through the airport. She was overwhelmed to discover that crowd was waiting for her.

The church also had a barbecue dinner waiting for her at church, where hundreds had gathered to welcome her back. At the conclusion of the evening, a special slideshow highlighted the years she spent in China, including video testimonies from many of the people she witnessed to and discipled. From housing to health care to home-cooked meals, the church was ready to welcome Daisy back.

With tears filling her eyes, Daisy said that she got a taste of heaven through the love, appreciation, and especially the preparation of the church in receiving her for retirement. What a beautiful display of grace and gratitude. I hope more missionaries will be celebrated in this way as a result of our love, care, and prayers.

DISCUSSION QUESTIONS

- Have you ever come home after a long period away and things felt different: maybe after going away to college or studying abroad? Share what you experienced and what you felt had changed when you returned home.

- What do you think are the biggest challenges your missionaries might face when coming home?

- What can your church do to help with the readjustments missionaries face when coming home?

PRAYER POINTS

- Pray that God would establish a culture of love, honor, and celebration when welcoming missionaries home.

- When your missionaries are on furlough or sabbatical, ask God to give them deep rest and restore their joy while they are with you.

- Pray that God would give them grace in readjusting to life back home.

ACTION PLAN

- Check to see the next time missionaries will be visiting your church and plan some special activities to make them feel loved and welcomed.

- When missionaries visit and give missions reports, encourage church members to come together to hear their updates and celebrate the work they are doing.

- When your missionaries come home to retire, plan a special retirement party for them, honoring them for their years of service.

12

Pray to End Well

1 PETER 5:5-14

IT'S NOT HOW YOU START but how you finish that counts. An older football coach said the following about a young, aspiring coach: "He doesn't seem to have much football knowledge and he lacks motivation." He was speaking of the great Vince Lombardi. (The Super Bowl trophy is named after him!) A newspaper editor was fired because "he lacked creative ideas." That man was Walt Disney. Thomas Edison was called "stupid" by teachers who gave up on him. Beethoven was called "hopeless to become a good composer." And Michael Jordan was cut from his junior high basketball team.[1]

It's not how we start and it's not how others view us that matters. What matters most is how we finish. It is a rare thing to finish well. In his study of leadership, Steve Farrar argues that we're fortunate to see even one in ten leaders finish strong.[2] A lot of people start off well, but what counts is how they end. So the crucial question for us is, "How do we finish well?"

Finishing well is difficult. Many who start off in ministry won't retire as a minister.[3] Finishing well is a challenge in life, in ministry, and in missions. Therefore, we want to pray that missionaries will finish their race well. So how should we pray for them?

STAY HUMBLE

To finish well, our missionaries need to stay humble before the Lord:

> You who are younger, be subject to the elders. Clothe yourselves, all of you, with humility toward one another, for "God opposes the proud but gives grace to the humble." Humble yourselves, therefore, under the mighty hand of God so that at the proper time he may exalt you, casting all your anxieties on him, because he cares for you. (1 Peter 5:5-7)

Peter is reminding us to honor God because our motives and methods matter to God. *What* we do is important, but *why* and *how* we do things are also important. He gives us this warning because he wants to protect our rewards in our service to God. When we do good things with the wrong motive, we risk losing our rewards for serving him. Although Peter was speaking to the leaders and servants of the first-century church, he is also speaking to everyone in the church, and he reminds us of the importance of staying humble in our relationships.

Repetition in Scripture stresses importance. Instead of making something bold or italicized, authors would repeat something in order to highlight an important message. And there are a couple of key things being repeated for us in 1 Peter 5.

First, he emphasizes the importance of submission to the elders in the church (v. 5). A general principle for our relationships to leaders is to submit to them, unless they ask us to sin. On top of that, our humility, love, and trust of Jesus will be seen in submitting to the leaders he has placed over us.

Peter is also repeating the need to stay humble (vv. 5-6). He says cover yourselves with an attitude of humility. This means putting others ahead of yourself and seeking to meet others' needs first. In other words, ask, *How can I serve someone here? How can I bless?*

Peter then gives a key reason for this attitude: The proud, who think of themselves first or who think they are better than others, are opposed by God (v. 5). Pride is ugly.

Ricky Henderson was a great baseball player who never said much. He was good at stealing bases, and his goal was to be the all-time base-stealing leader. Growing up, I actually admired him quite a bit. But after he broke the record, the game was paused so everyone could congratulate him. And he lifted the base and proclaimed, "I am the greatest! I am the greatest!" After that, it was hard to be his fan anymore. I realized that a quiet person isn't necessarily humble. Quietness doesn't tell us what's going on in our hearts.

That same ugliness lives in my own heart. I've written a number of praise songs since my high school days. The first time I introduced a song to my praise team during my seminary years, I couldn't wait for them to sing it. While we were practicing it, one person said they liked it, and I blurted out, "I wrote it!"

But the moment I said that, I sensed the Holy Spirit pointing out my pride. I never again sang one of my songs in church during my seminary years because I felt my pride couldn't handle it. An ugly monster had come out of my heart.

But not only is pride ugly, it's dangerous. Why? Pride puts me at the center of my life, where God alone must be. Pride says I am more important than you. It takes credit and glory for a self that belongs to God alone. Pride says, "I deserve the praise! Not God." It says, "Look at what I've done! Look at me! Admire me! Depend on me!" But all praise, glory, and honor belong to Christ alone.

Peter tells us that God opposes the proud, but he pours out grace to the humble (v. 5). We not only need God's grace to save us, we need it to sustain us so we can live in this fallen world and honor him through it all.

In verse 6, Peter says to let God do the exalting, not us. Let God do the honoring; don't seek it for ourselves. Verse 7 also reveals another element of humility; we are to cast our anxieties on him, because he cares for us. When we trust Christ, we know he will take care of us.

Surrender your worries to God because they can be a sign of pride. Worry suggests that our problems are more powerful than God. Worry reveals that sometimes we don't trust God, therefore we have to take care of ourselves. But faith is a sign of humility, for faith believes that God knows what he is doing. So we want to pray that our missionaries' hearts will be humble, not hard.

STAY WATCHFUL

For our missionaries to finish well, we also must pray that they will be watchful. Peter says, "Be sober-minded; be *watchful*. Your adversary the devil prowls around like a roaring lion, seeking someone to devour" (1 Peter 5:8, emphasis mine). If you want to finish your life well, you need to remember that life is war. We are in a fight, a spiritual battle for our souls. Our enemy is seeking someone to kill! Destroy! Devour! This is the life of a missionary, and we must pray they never forget that the struggles we face are warfare for our faith!

Paul reminds us in Ephesians 6:12, "We do not wrestle against flesh and blood, but against the rulers, against the authorities, against the cosmic powers over this present darkness, against the spiritual forces of evil in the heavenly places." Ultimately, our struggles are in the spiritual realm. Our real enemies are not mere people but principalities in the heavenly places. We like to demonize people we have conflicts with, but we must remember that humans are not the enemy.

The enemy will use people to hurt or harden our hearts, but God is using those situations to reveal the condition of our hearts, so stay watchful. Pray that the hearts of our missionaries will stay soft, humble, and forgiving. Pray that they will see their difficult circumstances with spiritual eyes and hearts of faith. And pray that they will keep fighting the good fight. Toward the end of his life, Paul says, "I have fought the good fight, I have finished the race, I have kept the faith" (2 Timothy 4:7). Pray this verse into the lives of our missionaries, that they would stay watchful to how the enemy attacks relationships.

All attacks of the enemy are attacks on our faith. Speaking of the devil, Peter says, "Resist him, firm in your faith, knowing that the same kinds of suffering are being experienced by your brotherhood throughout the world" (1 Peter 5:9). All believers go through suffering, which is a refining process so our faith will be purified as gold in the end.

I once heard a story of a boy stuck in his room late at night when a fire blazed through his family's house. As smoke filled his room, he heard the scream of his dad outside. The son looked out his window and could hear his dad but couldn't see him because of the smoke and darkness. The dad screamed to his son to jump out the window.

The son replied, "But, Dad, I'm on the second floor, and I can't see you!"

The dad replied, "That's okay, son, because I can see you!"

This is a great reminder that faith is not about seeing God but believing that I am seen by him. Faith is believing that though I cannot see my father in heaven, I know he sees exactly where I am right now. And his arms are open wide to receive me and catch me when I fall.

We need to be reminded that we are not suffering alone. Saints around the world are also suffering. But even more than that, the God who loves us suffered for us as well. He is Immanuel: *God with us* (Matthew 1:23). He is with us, especially in our pain. God is with us always. Our missionaries need to be reminded of this truth as they carry their crosses and follow Jesus. This is part of staying watchful to the tactics of the enemy against our faith, especially in times of suffering.

One of the ways we can counter the attacks of the enemy in our watchfulness is to worship because worship is a powerful weapon that puts the focus on Almighty God in the midst of warfare. A leader who has faced much spiritual warfare observes,

> Praise is an act of faith that affirms the character and redemptive power of God in all circumstances. If God truly dwells in the praises of his people, the regular practice of praise must be built into the lifestyle of the spiritual warrior. I used to feel weighed down by the burden of spiritual battles, but then I learned a secret. God waits for us to praise him so he can pour out his strength in us. Praise releases divine power.[4]

So in the midst of spiritual battles, faith will be strengthened by a heart that worships while staying watchful.

STAY HOPEFUL

In order for our missionaries to finish well, we must also pray that they stay hopeful. Peter says, "After you have suffered a little while, the God of all grace, who has called you to his eternal glory in Christ, will himself restore, confirm, strengthen, and establish you. To him be the dominion forever and ever. Amen" (1 Peter 5:10-11). Our suffering will not last forever. Compared to the eternal rest we will enter, our suffering lasts only "a little while." After our short time of suffering, the God of all grace (that's the sum of our lives: grace!), who has called us to his eternal glory in Christ (that is our destiny!), will restore us. Everything that was ruined because of sin will be restored. Because of this truth, we are a people of hope. There are greater days ahead, and our missionaries need to be reminded of this truth repeatedly.

C. S. Lewis said,

> Hope is one of the theological virtues. This means that a continual looking forward to the eternal world is not a form of escapism or wishful thinking, but one of the things a Christian is meant to do. It does not mean that we are to leave the present world as it is. If you read history, you will find that the Christians who did most for the present world were just those who thought most of the next.[5]

We are a people of hope because our life and destiny are in the hands of God Almighty, who controls the universe. Because we know our end is secure, we can live this life with reckless abandon and pursue Christ and his kingdom with all our might. I love the last part of what Lewis said, "The Christians who did most for the present world were just those who thought most of the next." So let's pray that our missionaries always fix their eyes on the eternal kingdom, which will allow them to do their best to witness to God's kingdom.

I have met many discouraged missionaries who wonder if their lives have made a difference. And I know some who have made mistakes on the mission field, leaving them to wonder if they have failed completely. We must remind them that we are a people of hope. Part of that hope is knowing that our past does not equal our future. Our past may be filled with shame, but in Christ, our future is clothed with honor. Our past may be filled with regrets, but our future in Christ will be redeemed. A better life, a better world, is coming for all who are in Christ. The best is yet to come. This is not just truth to believe but our future hope. So pray that our missionaries would remain hopeful and hope-filled.

STAY LOVING

Finally, in order for our missionaries to finish well, we must pray that they will stay loving. Peter says,

> I have written briefly to you, exhorting and declaring that this is the true grace of God. Stand firm in it. She who is at Babylon, who is likewise chosen, sends you greetings, and so does Mark, my son. Greet one another with the kiss of love. Peace to all of you who are in Christ. (1 Peter 5:12-14)

Peter ends with love. He has stressed the importance of staying humble and watchful by guarding our faith. He's also stressed the importance of looking to the end and guarding our hope. And he ends with love. These are the three that remain: faith, hope, and love. "But the greatest of these is love" (1 Corinthians 13:13). Life is designed for loving God and each other. Pray that our missionaries never forget this. We are able to love because God first loved us. Jesus loved us so much that he extended grace upon grace to our lives, to save us from our sins so that we could be with him forever. And those who have received much mercy and grace gladly give that same mercy and grace to others.

Having pastored in South Korea for a total of over eleven years, one of my greatest honors has been meeting and ministering to North Koreans. It always amazes me to hear how many North Korean believers want to return to North Korea as missionaries. Even though they faced extreme hardships, such as poverty and prison, the love they have for their people has been placed in their hearts by the grace of God. It is a testimony to the Spirit's work in their lives that the hardships they faced did not harden their hearts.

One powerful example of this love was shared by Michael Oh, global executive director of the Lausanne Movement, at the Third Lausanne Congress at Cape Town.

On the second night of the Third Lausanne Congress taking place in Cape Town, South Africa, an 18 year-old girl from North Korea shared her story.

[This girl's father was very wealthy and worked as an assistant to the North Korean leader, Kim Jong II. Later on, because of increased difficulties, their entire family escaped to China.]

In China a relative brought her family to church where her parents came to know Jesus Christ. A few months later, however, her pregnant mother died from Leukemia. Her father started to study the Bible with missionaries and eventually the Lord gave him a strong desire to become a missionary to North Korea. But in 2001 he was reported as a Christian, was arrested by the Chinese police, and was returned to North Korea. Forced to leave his daughter behind in China, he spent three years in prison. During this time the girl shared that it only "made my father's faith stronger" and that he "cried out to God more desperately rather than complain or blame Him."

After three years he was able to return to China where he was briefly reunited with his daughter. Soon after, however, he gathered Bibles having resolved to return to North Korea to share Christ among that hopeless people. He was given the opportunity to go to South Korea, but he turned them down.

In 2006 he was discovered by the North Korean government and was arrested. There has since been no word from him. In all probability he has been shot to death publicly for treason.

In 2007 this girl, who at the time was not a Christian, was given the opportunity to go to South Korea. While still in China waiting at the Korean Consulate in Beijing to go to South Korea, she saw Jesus in a dream. Jesus, with tears in his eyes, called her by name and said, "How much longer are you going to keep me waiting? Walk with me. Yes, you lost your earthly father, but I am your heavenly Father and whatever has happened to you is because I love you."

She knelt and prayed to God for the first time and realized that "God my Father loves and cares for me so very much that He sent His Son Jesus to die for me." She prayed, "God here I am. I just lay down everything and give you my heart, my soul, my mind, and my strength. Please use me as you will."

Now God has given her a great love for North Korea. She shared that, "Just as my father was used there for God's kingdom, I now desire to be obedient to God. I want to bring the love of Jesus to North Korea."

She closed with the following words:

> I look back over my short life and see God's hand everywhere. Six years in North Korea, 11 years in China, and a time of being in South Korea. Everything that I experienced and love, I want to give it all to God and use my life for His kingdom. I hope to honor my father and bring glory to my heavenly Father by serving God with my whole heart.
>
> I believe God's heart cries out for the lost people of North Korea. I humbly ask you, my brothers and sisters, to have the same heart of God. Please pray that the same light of God's grace and mercy that reached my father and my mother and now me will one day come down upon the people of North Korea . . . my people.[6]

She had every reason to hate North Korea and to never want to go back. But instead of being overcome by evil, God empowered her to overcome evil with good. This is something we cannot do in our own strength. When people hurt us, curse us, and even harm us, it's so easy for our hearts to grow cold. This is a challenge for all believers in our day-to-day living. But this is a great challenge for missionaries and ministers who have experienced hurts and betrayals from people they have dedicated their lives to love. It's easy to harden our hearts, grow bitter, and cut these people out of our lives. It takes divine grace to keep caring for those who don't care about us.

I want to share one more story about a couple whose work has influenced me to this day. I've been praying for the persecuted church around the world through the stories that are shared by Voice of the Martyrs. One of the founders of this ministry, Richard Wurmbrand, was a pastor in Romania who spent fourteen years in jail for speaking out against communism. In 1945, after the communists took control of Romania, he began a ministry to the underground believers who also opposed the new leadership.

In 1948, Richard and his wife, Sabina, were arrested, and Richard spent the first three years of his imprisonment in solitary confinement. But even after he was released to a group cell, his torture continued. Day after day he was beaten and abused while his torturers screamed at him, demanding that he deny Christ and renounce his faith. Through it all, he remained faithful to Christ and became a witness even in his prison.

He was finally released from jail, and soon thereafter he and his wife went to the United States and testified before the

US Senate Internal Security Subcommittee about the torture he endured under the communist regime. He took off his shirt to show eighteen scars from the devastating blows to his torso. His story was told in news outlets throughout the United States, Europe, and Asia. He was threatened by the Romanian government and was told that if he did not stay quiet, there would be deadly consequences. But Richard remained firm in his faith and in his message to the global church to pray for those around the world persecuted for their faith.

This led to the formation of Voice of the Martyrs, a ministry that brings the urgent needs of the mission field and the persecuted church to the global church. Richard died at the age of ninety-one on February 17, 2001. His message has always been, "Hate the evil systems, but love your persecutors. Love their souls, and try to win them for Christ."[7]

Let's pray that our missionaries will finish their race with love in their hearts. As Romans 13:8 reminds us, "Let no debt remain outstanding, except the continuing debt to love one another, for whoever loves others has fulfilled the law" (NIV). Pray that love will be the lasting mark of our missionaries' work in the nations. Pray that love will be the aim of their lives, for that is the only guaranteed way to finish their race well.

DISCUSSION QUESTIONS

- Why do you think it's so hard for people to finish well?

- What are some factors that can help us finish well?

- How do you think hope in the future promises of Christ helps us in finishing well?

PRAYER POINTS

- Ask God to keep the hearts of your missionaries soft, humble, and hungry for the Lord.

- Ask God to fill their hearts with promises of what is coming at the redemption of all things, putting their hope in Christ and his kingdom.

- Pray that they will stay loving toward all those they serve, even those who have hurt them.

ACTION PLAN

- Buy a map, put it on your wall at home, and place sticker dots in every city where you have missionaries you support. Place the missionary's name and photo near that city. Let it become a daily visual reminder to pray for them and their countries.

- Set aside a set amount or set percentage of money that you will give to missions work each month.

- If you have children, give them a piggy bank in which they too can learn to set aside a portion of their money for missions work.

Epilogue

LET'S FINISH THE MISSION
AND GO HOME

JIM ELLIOT IS OFTEN LIFTED UP in Christian circles as a true hero in the world of missions, and rightly so. He epitomizes what we envision when we think of surrendering our lives for the mission field—and becoming a martyr for Christ. Jim, along with four others, died at hands of tribal warriors in Ecuador in 1956. These warriors were the very people they were trying to reach with the gospel. We also celebrate God's grace in the fruit of their deaths, as we later discover that many from that tribe eventually became believers.

But another story I love concerns the life and testimony of Jim's brother, Bert, who isn't well-known, but who finished his race just as faithfully as his famous brother. Bert and his wife, Colleen, were students at Multnomah Bible College in 1949 when they were invited to become missionaries to Peru, many years before Jim went to Ecuador. They faithfully served the people of Peru for over sixty years. Regarding

Bert's ministry, Randy Alcorn says, "They may have served Christ faithfully under the radar of the church at large, but not under God's."

In speaking of his brother, Bert once said, "Jim and I both served Christ, but differently. Jim was a great meteor, streaking through the sky." Alcorn followed up that comment by saying that Bert was a "faint star that rose night after night, faithfully crossing the same path in the sky, to God's glory."

Alcorn then reflected on Bert's life with these poignant words:

> In missions work, suffering sometimes results in a short life culminating in martyrdom, sometimes in a long life of daily dying to self and living for Christ. I believe Jim Elliot's reward is considerable, but it wouldn't surprise me to discover that Bert and Colleen's will be greater still. . . . Bert and Colleen Elliot have lived a long obedience in the same direction. Whether we follow God to leave our country or to stay here, all of us are likewise called to a life of faithful endurance, empowered by Christ.[1]

I love Bert's story because it reminds me of my story. A simple life of obedience motivated by love for God. His life wasn't applauded by crowds. He didn't become a celebrity preacher. He simply followed Jesus and shared the gospel wherever God sent him. His aim wasn't fame but faithfulness. I hope that's how I will finish too—faithful.

The mission field can be a lonely place. I've heard too many places referred to as a "missions graveyard." These are places where people come in with great zeal for the nations and great passion for the lost, but after years of difficulties and spiritual drought, they go home defeated, deflated, and discouraged. Far too many missionaries feel as if they are fighting alone on the mission field. I want to change that through the prayers of this book. I want to see missionaries strengthened because the church is coming alive in intercessory prayer and compassionate care for their missionaries. I want to see prayers increase for the mission field to such an extent in our generation that we will see the completion of the Great Commission in our lifetime. Jesus told us to pray that God would send out workers into his harvest fields. I want to see churches praying, fasting, sending, and supporting missions work more than any other generation has before.

The more prayers we can release into the mission field, the greater the harvest will be. Jesus says there is a direct correlation between the gospel reaching the nations and his return. Because I want to see Jesus, I want to finish the mission he gave us. So let's commit to praying for all the peoples of the world to know the name of Jesus. Let's commit to praying for our missionaries to remain in Jesus and to be faithful till the end. Let's finish the mission and go home.

Church, let's do this.

DISCUSSION QUESTIONS

- How does the sentence "Let's finish the mission and go home" make you feel? What is at heart behind it?

- How do you think your role in global missions will change now that you've read this book?

- What was the biggest takeaway after reading this book?

PRAYER POINTS

- Ask God to increase your prayers, your giving, and your involvement in global missions.

- Ask God to use your life and your church to strengthen missions work around the world.

- Ask God to finish the mission in your lifetime.

ACTION PLAN

- Consider adopting a people group that needs to know Jesus, and commit to praying, fasting, giving, and going to serve that people group.

- Call or write and bless a missionary today.

- Give copies of this book, along with prayer cards or news-letters of your missionaries, to others who you can recruit as intercessors. One of the greatest gifts you can give your missionaries is increasing prayer for them.

Acknowledgments

THANK YOU, JESUS, for being a missionary God. Thank you, James Mackenzie, for coming to South Korea as a missionary and bringing the gospel to my great-great-grandfather many years ago. I look forward to thanking you in person when I enter glory. Thank you to the many faithful missionaries who gave their lives to bring the gospel to Korea. I was able to write this book because of their obedience. Thank you to my grandfather Sung Hak Byun for praying so faithfully for every one of your children, grandchildren, and great-grandchildren. I am forever the fruit of your prayers. Thank you, Mom and Dad, for raising us in a church that preached the gospel. Thank you, Rev. David Yang, for being a faithful shepherd when I first came to know the Lord at the age of twelve. Thank you, Rev. "Master" Yang, for faithfully preaching what it means to be born again at my very first retreat. I will never forget that night in Michigan when everyone in our youth group gave their life to Jesus. My life and my eternity will never be the same as a result.

Thank you, Hyun, for your faithful presence and support throughout every season and every year of our marriage. I love you so much. Thank you, Enoch, for teaching me what it means to trust in the Father's love. Thank you, Emma, for pushing me to pray and fast like never before.

Thank you, Don and the Gates Group, for believing in this project and the continual support you've provided every step of the way. Thank you, Al and the team at InterVarsity Press. It's always an honor and delight to work with you on my book projects. Thank you, Charse Yun and Daniel Downey, for lending your time, talents, and eye for details in some of the edits for this book. Thank you, Eunice Yun, Aejin Kim, and the team at Kyujang, for your prayers, help, and support for the Korean version of this book.

Thank you, Pastor Min Chung, for keeping missions so central during my university years at Covenant Fellowship Church. It made a lasting impact on my life. Thank you to my many friends on the mission field who obeyed Jesus' call to go to the nations. Great is your reward in heaven.

Thank you to the precious partners in the Lausanne Movement, Frontiers, Pioneers, Voice of the Martyrs, Operation Mobilization, Overseas Missionary Fellowship, Agape International Missions, Ratanak, Liberty in North Korea, International House of Prayer in Kansas City, Youth With a Mission, Five Two Foundation, Reah International, the Nehemiah Community, Footstool Missions Center, and many others who are praying for missions, preparing missionaries, sending out workers, and supporting global missions around the world. God bless the work of your hands.

Thank you, Pastor Ha and Mrs. Ha, for pioneering the Acts 29 vision for Onnuri, OEM, and for this generation.

Thank you to those who served with me on missions at Midwest Church, CFC, Handong International Church, Seasoon, New Life, OEM, HOPE Be Restored, Crossway Mission Church, and Venture Christian Church.

Thank you to my faithful intercessors at Crossway Mission Church, OEM, HOPE Be Restored, Kingdom First, New Philly, Jubilee Church, and Venture Christian Church.

Notes

1 PRAY FOR MORE WORKERS TO FINISH THE MISSION

[1]The Joshua Project, accessed May 1, 2018, www.joshuaproject.net; and "Has Everyone Heard?," Joshua Project, accessed May 1, 2018, https://joshua project.net/resources/articles/has_everyone_heard.

[2]"Missions Stats: The Current State of the World," Traveling Team, accessed May 1, 2018, www.thetravelingteam.org/stats.

[3]"What Is the 10/40 Window?," Joshua Project, accessed May 1, 2018, https://joshuaproject.net/resources/articles/10_40_window.

[4]"10/40 Window to 4/14 Window," Promise Church, accessed May 1, 2018, www.promise414.com/414-window/1040-window-to-414-window.

[5]Randy Alcorn, *Money, Possessions, and Eternity* (Carol Stream, IL: Tyndale House, 1989), 291; and Richard Stearns, *The Hole in Our Gospel: What Does God Expect of Us? The Answer That Changed My Life and Might Just Change the World* (Nashville: Thomas Nelson, 2009), 216.

[6]John Piper, *Desiring God: Meditations of a Christian Hedonist*, rev. ed. (Colorado Springs: Multnomah Press, 2011), 178.

[7]Jason Mandryk, *Operation World: The Definitive Prayer Guide for Every Nation* (Downers Grove, IL: InterVarsity Press, 2010).

2 PRAY FOR INTIMACY WITH GOD

[1]Brian Pruett and Bailey Pruett, "Just How Stressed Are Missionaries (and What Can We Do About It)?," *Ethnos 360*, March 23, 2012, http://blogs .ntm.org/brian-pruett/2012/03/23/just-how-stressed-are-missionaries -and-what-can-we-do-about-it.

[2]Chery Flores, "The 5 Types of Stress Every Missionary Faces," *MTW*, May 13, 2015, www.mtw.org/stories/details/5-types-of-stress-every-missionary -faces.

[3]Ronald L. Koteskey, "What Missionaries Ought to Know About Culture Stress," *Missionary Care*, accessed May 1, 2018, www.missionarycare.com /culture-stress.html.

[4]Taylor William, *Too Valuable to Lose: Exploring the Causes and Cures of Missionary Attrition* (Pasadena, CA: William Carey Library, 2013), 13.

[5]J. Russell Turney, *Leave a Legacy: Increasing Missionary Longevity* (Eugene, OR: Wipf & Stock, 2017), 11.

[6]John Piper, *Let the Nations Be Glad: The Supremacy of God in Missions* (Grand Rapids: Baker Academic, 2003), 17.

[7]David Brainerd, quoted in Jonathan Edwards, *The Life of David Brainerd*, ed. Norman Pettit, Works of Jonathan Edwards 7 (New Haven, CT: Yale University Press, 1985), 474.

3 PRAY FOR SPIRITUAL COVERAGE

[1]Billy Graham, *Angels: God's Secret Agents* (Nashville: Thomas Nelson, 2011), 3.

[2]Jim Elliot, quoted in Elizabeth Elliot, *Shadow of the Almighty: The Life and Testament of Jim Elliot* (Peabody, MA: Hendrickson, 2008), 15.

[3]Ted Limpic, "Brazilian Missionaries: How Long Are They Staying?," in *Too Valuable to Lose: Exploring the Causes and Cures of Missionary Attrition*, ed. William D. Taylor (Pasadena, CA: William Carey Library, 2013), 147.

4 PRAY FOR STRONG SINGLES, MARRIAGES, AND FAMILIES

[1]Lisa Beth White, "Carmichael, Amy Beatrice (1867–1951)," Boston University, accessed May 1, 2015, www.bu.edu/missiology/missionary -biography/c-d/carmichael-amy-beatrice-1867-1951.

[2]Rachael Green, "The 9 Gifts Third Culture Kids Bring to Missions," Urbana .org, June 1, 2016, https://urbana.org/blog/9-gifts-third-culture-kids-bring -missions.

[3]David Pollock and Ruth Van Reken, *Third Culture Kids: Growing Up Among Worlds* (Boston: Nicholas Brealey, 2010), 13.

[4]Peter Scazzero, *The Emotionally Healthy Leader: How Transforming Your Inner Life Will Deeply Transform Your Church, Team, and the World* (Grand Rapids: Zondervan, 2015), 82.

5 PRAY FOR INCARNATIONAL LOVE
FOR THE NATIONS

[1]Ida Horner, "Dear 'Dancing Missionaries' You Are Still Offensive to Africans," *Guardian*, October 14, 2016, www.theguardian.com/world/2016 /oct/14/dancing-missionaries-white-girls-offensive-to-africans.

[2]According to the UNHCR, "the international legal definition of a stateless person is 'a person who is not considered as a national by any State under the operation of its law.' In simple terms, this means that a stateless person does not have a nationality of any country." Some people are born stateless, but others become stateless. See "Ending Statelessness," UNHCR, accessed June 15, 2018, www.unhcr.org/en-us/stateless-people.html.

6 PRAY FOR ONENESS IN THE TEAMS

[1]Mother Teresa, *In My Own Words* (Barnhart, MO: Liguori, 1996), 53.

7 PRAY FOR NEVER-ENDING DEVOTION

[1]John H. Sammis, "Trust and Obey," 1887.

8 PRAY FOR SUCCESSFUL MINISTRY
IN THE EYES OF GOD

[1]Olivia Blair, "Staying Off Facebook Can Make You Happier, Study Claims," *Independent*, November 10, 2015, www.independent.co.uk/life-style /gadgets-and-tech/news/staying-off-facebook-can-make-you-happier -study-claims-a6728056.html.

9 PRAY FOR CHURCHES
TO PARTNER WELL

[1]Rick Warren, quoted in Richard Abanes, *Rick Warren and the Purpose That Drives Him* (Eugene, OR: Harvest House, 2005), 32.

11 PRAY FOR REENTERING WELL

[1]Peter Scazzero, *The Emotionally Healthy Leader: How Transforming Your Inner Life Will Deeply Transform Your Church, Team, and the World* (Grand Rapids: Zondervan, 2015), 25.

12 PRAY TO END WELL

[1]*Daily Grace for Teens* (Colorado Springs: David C. Cook, 2013), 34.

[2]Steve Farrar, *Finishing Strong: Going the Distance for Your Family* (New York: Crown Publishing, 2011), 19.

[3]Eddie Byun, *Praying for Your Pastor: How Your Prayer Support Is Their Life Support* (Downers Grove, IL: InterVarsity Press, 2016), 20.

[4]Thomas B. White, *The Believer's Guide to Spiritual Warfare* (Ann Arbor, MI: Servant, 2011), 64

[5]C. S. Lewis, quoted in Grayson Carter, *Sehnsucht: The C. S. Lewis Journal* (Eugene, OR: Wipf & Stock, 2009), 2:44.

[6]Michael Oh, "Weeping for North Korea," *Desiring God*, October 19, 2010, www.desiringgod.org/articles/weeping-for-north-korea.

[7]"Our Founders," Voice of the Martyrs, accessed May 1, 2015, www.perse cution.com/founders.

EPILOGUE: LET'S FINISH
THE MISSION AND GO HOME

[1]Randy Alcorn, "Bert Elliot: A Faithful Star, Rising Night After Night for Christ," Eternal Perspective Ministries, February 19, 2012, www.epm.org /blog/2012/Feb/19/bert-elliot-faithful-star-rising-night-after-night.

About the Author

Eddie Byun resides in San Jose, California, with his wife, Hyun, and son, Enoch. He is currently the missions and teaching pastor of Venture Christian Church in Los Gatos, California. He previously taught practical theology at Torch Trinity Graduate University and has been lead pastor for Crossway Mission Church and Onnuri English Ministry in Seoul, South Korea. He has also pastored in Sydney, Australia, and Vancouver, Canada. He is the author of *Justice Awakening*, which won the Reader's Choice Award, and *Praying for Your Pastor*. He was also the executive producer of *Save My Seoul*, an award-winning documentary on sex trafficking in South Korea.

Email: eddie2024@gmail.com
Website: eddiebyun.com

Also by Eddie Byun

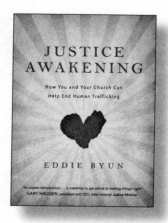

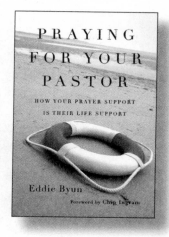